Contents (Fifth Edition)

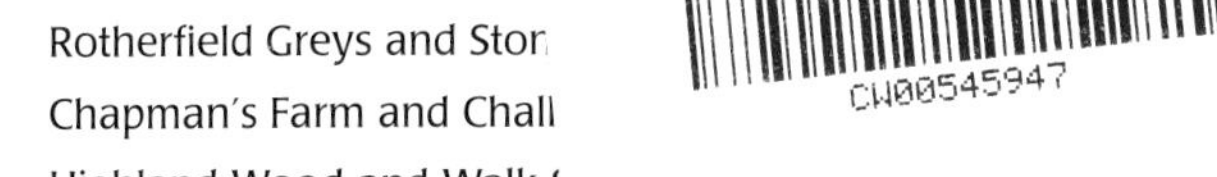

1 Gillsmithers Wood and Dr
2 Rotherfield Greys and Stor
3 Chapman's Farm and Chall
4 Highland Wood and Walk
5 Nuney Green and Path Hill ..... 4 miles
6 Whitchurch Hill and Boze Down ⇌ ⊖ ..... 5 miles
7 Pangbourne College and River Pang ⇌ ⊖ ..... 5 miles
8 Moor Copse and Sulham Woods ⊖ ..... 3¼ miles
9 North Street and Englefield Estate ⇌ ⊖ ..... 4 miles
10 Kiln Pond and Simms Copse ⊖ ..... 4 miles
11 Ufton Court and Seward's Gully ..... 4 miles
12 Ufton Green and Padworth House ⇌ ⊖ ..... 4, 5½ or 6 miles
13 Roman Amphitheatre and Foudry Brook ⊖ ..... 5 miles
14 Grazeley Church and Hopkiln Farm ..... 3¾ miles
15 Devil's Highway and Beech Hill ⇌ ..... 5¾ miles
16 Shinfield and Three Mile Cross ⊖ ..... 4¾ miles
17 Swallowfield Park and Thatcher's Ford ⊖ ..... 4 or 6½ miles
18 Pudding Lane and Farley Hill ⊖ ..... 4½ miles
19 Fleet Copse and Rectory Farm ⊖ ..... 5 or 5½ miles
20 Hatch Farm and Loaders Lane ..... 2½ miles
21 Theale Lake and Whitehouse Green ⊖ ..... 5¼ to 6 miles
22 Milkmaid's Bridge and Holy Brook ⊖ ..... 4 miles
23 Chill Hill and Jouldings Farm ..... 5 miles
24 Lower Shiplake and the Lock ⇌ ⊖ ..... 2¾ or 3¾ miles

The Ramblers' Association promotes country walking and protects rights of way. Having successfully campaigned in recent years for access to open country and Forestry Commission woodland, we now have our sights set on securing public access to remaining stretches of the coast of England and Wales. The RA plays a major role in securing legislation to protect our paths and countryside. Please give your support by becoming a member.
Write to: The Ramblers' Association, Camelford House, 87-90 Albert Embankment, London SE1 7TW Tel: 020 73398500 Website: www.ramblers.org.uk

Berkshire Area
The RA has seven Groups across the County. Each Group arranges its own programme of walks and endeavours to monitor local footpaths, to seek improvements and oppose any threats to them. For details contact:
Mr John Moules, 50 Qualitas, Roman Hill, Bracknell, Berkshire RG12 7QG.

Gillsmithers Wood and Drawback Hill

This circular route enjoys a popular stretch of the River Thames (a National Trail) before climbing up into the beautiful Chiltern Hills surrounding Henley-on-Thames. The distance is reduced by a mile if starting from the car park near Marsh Lock.

Distance: 8 (or 7) miles
OS Map: Explorer 171 Chiltern Hills West
Start: Henley-on-Thames station or car park at Mill Lane.*
(Grid ref: 771 817)

Half-way house... The 'Bottle & Glass'

Leaving station entrance, turn right down Station Road to River Thames at Hobbs boatyard, then turn right along towpath for about ¾ mile (passing River & Rowing Museum). Where the riverside path reaches start of footbridge to Marsh Lock, turn away from river, up narrow road (Mill Lane). After car park* (alternative start) continue over railway bridge and with care cross Reading Road (A4155) into Nobel Road opposite. Follow left-hand footway and where road turns right, go straight on up gravel bridleway. Cross road ahead and continue up Peppard Lane, using raised footway at first, then passing several road ends on right. Eventually, where made-up road finishes by Cilgerran House, continue ahead on hedged bridleway with field on left.

1 At junction of paths continue slightly right into broad fenced path and shortly cross road to enter area of public open space through kissing gate on left. Follow hedge on right to second gate then continue on grass verge of Greys Road to reach and turn left into Highlands Lane. After two pairs of houses on right, turn right into short grass strip, then head across open field to wide gap in hedge, just left of trees. Turn half-left through middle of next field and at solitary tree in the middle, ignore right-hand fork and aim for gap in far boundary. Here continue on wide grass path between fences, cross stile after tarmac drive and head down middle of two fields to reach stile into lane, close to white-painted Old Place. Now turn right along road for about 30 yards and then sharp left up woodland path through Gillsmithers Wood.

2 After passing North Lodge of Crowsley Park, keep straight on until park railings finally bend right and the path bears left, down through woodland. Disregard both a path forking right off the descent and a further crossing track just after bottom of hollow (neither are rights of way). As path starts to rise, go right at a fork and continue climbing path between low banks. On emerging from woods bear right to follow sunken path (Bones Lane) along right-hand edge of field. On reaching the 'Bottle & Glass', turn left along road for about ¼ mile to turn right into bridleway at near corner of High Wood. After metal gate just ahead, follow broad track through middle of wood; the line winding through younger trees on far side.

3 Emerging from woods keep straight on along gravel drive beside paddock for about 60 yards, then cross stile on left. Follow edge of field with

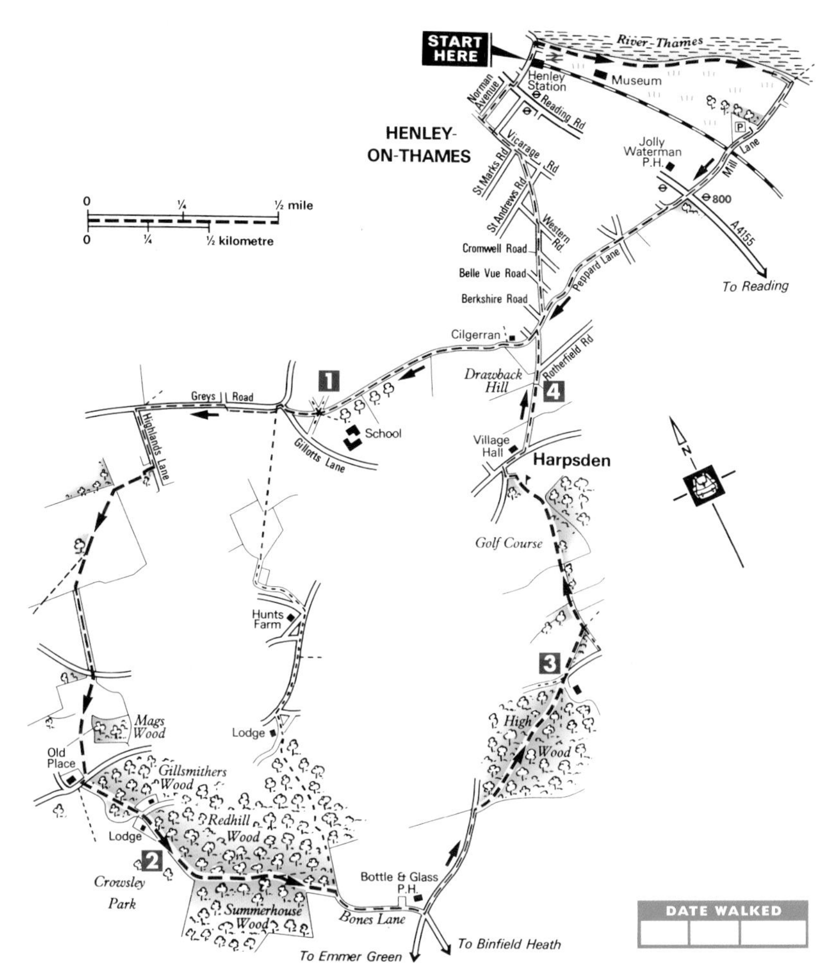

fence on right but do not pass over stile ahead, instead turn left along edge of same field and after another stile continue still beside fence on right. After further stile keep straight ahead over golf course, following green marker posts leading down a grass track. When level with corner of copse on right, bear slightly left across course then down slope and left along short track leading to road. Turn right and at junction, facing barn, right again, through Harpsden village. Immediately after last house on left, turn left into fenced path and climb steep left side of field known as Drawback Hill.

4 Shortly after stile at top of climb, pass across end of road (Rotherfield Road) into narrow fenced path ahead. At end of this path turn right for 100 yards. Here is the choice of return routes. For those going to Mill Lane retrace your steps down Peppard Lane; for those going to the station fork left into fenced path leading straight down between houses. Path follows Cromwell Road for a stretch, then at junction with Western Road goes left for 15 yards before continuing down two further fenced sections, before turning left (along Vicarage Road) by pillar box. Where this road bends right, keep straight on past school on left, then turn right down hedged path to cross main road (A4155) and along Station Road back to start.

Rotherfield Greys and Stony Bottom

This delightful walk, in the area between modern Sonning Common and historic Henley-on-Thames, passes through a typical Chiltern landscape of tidy fields, wooded slopes, old farmhouses and venerable village churches.

Distance: 4½ miles
OS Map: Explorer 171 Chiltern Hills West
Start: Lay-by in Peppard Road (B481) opposite St Michael's Church, Sonning Common. (Grid ref: 708 807)

Facing the Catholic Church, turn left along road (B481) and at crossroads by end of bungalows, turn left up Widmore Lane, then after Widmore Pond turn right along Blountscourt Road for about ¼ mile. Some 200 yards beyond Blounts Farm, turn left on footpath signed 'Henley-on-Thames 2' and go ahead to near end of hedge, then maintain same direction diagonally through middle of large field, towards left-hand end of woodland on right. Continue down right-hand side of next field to enter trees in valley bottom. Here, keep close to fence on right and climb steep path ahead. Enter field near top of climb and continue with hedge on right.

1 Just before end of field, continue on fenced path, emerging in lane by red-brick house. Here turn left (Kings Farm Lane) and shortly, at left-hand bend facing pair of cottages, bear right, over stile next to gate. After some 40 yards along gravel track turn left, cross stile in hedge-gap. Follow fenced path between paddocks to opening in tree-lined field boundary. Continue ahead, on track between fields leading to Cowfields Farm. Go on, through wooden field-gate and just ahead, at footpath junction, turn half-left through middle of field to gap in hedge at road junction. Now keep straight on along road ahead to Rotherfield Greys.

Arriving in hamlet, note on left Pear Tree Cottages, built about 1500 and now in the safe keeping of Henley Housing Trust (see board). On right, a little building commemorates Queen Victoria's Diamond Jubilee in 1897 (see inscription over doorway). Down the years this has served as both well-house and bus-stop!

2 Immediately after the attractive part-17th century church of St Nicholas,

Stony Bottom

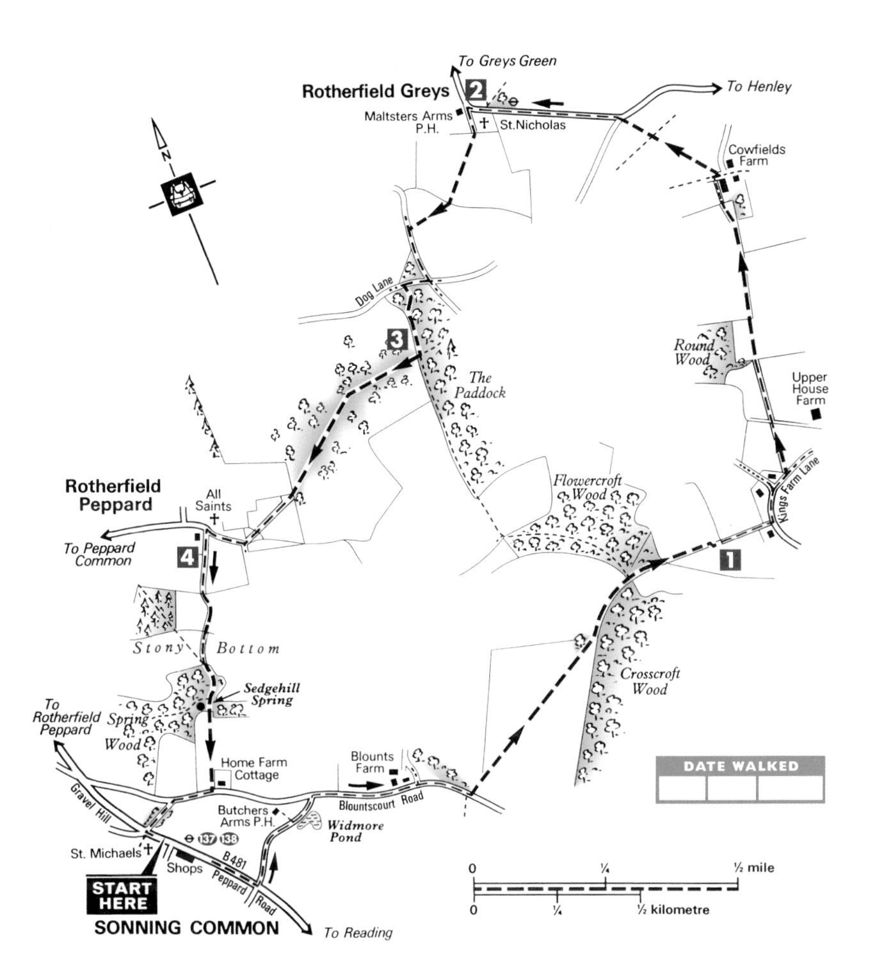

turn left into narrow path beside churchyard and after gate ahead, go half-right through paddock and middle of two fields, with gate between, then turn left along hedged bridleway. After passing through wooden swing-gate turn right down gravel track (Dog Lane). Nearing end of woodland on left, turn left through metal swing-gate into path along edge of woodland.

3 After almost 300 yards, at path junction, turn right through gate to follow the wide grass strip ahead, through an area of young trees. At top of slope keep to broad track, soon going down and up again, to reach stile on far side, just beyond an oak tree. From here enter fenced path between paddocks. After low stile, turn right into drive leading to, on right, Parish Church of All Saints, Rotherfield Peppard.

4 Immediately before first house on left, turn left into narrow path beside fields. After kissing gate at end of fenced section keep close to bushes on right as path descends steeply towards Stony Bottom. From gate in field corner definitive path crosses valley bottom beside fence on right, then climb up through trees, passing Sedgehill Spring on right. At top of slope go straight on across field and turn right along road. After some 200 yards bear left, by Highwood House, into fenced footpath leading down steps to road. Here turn left to return to start.

Chapman's Farm and Chalkhouse Green

A scenic circuit on well-used high ground Chiltern tracks and field-paths, much of which is across the well-farmed acres of the Coppid Hall estate. Built up by the Philimore family since 1855, the farms today cover some 2,500 acres, (including about 500 acres of woodland) in the parishes of Eye & Dunsden and Shiplake.

Distance: 5½ miles
OS Map: Explorer 159 Reading
Start: Playing-field car park, top of Caversham Park Road. (Grid ref: 726 768)

From car park entrance, turn left along broad grass verge. Shortly, directly opposite Northbrook Road, fork left into tree-lined footpath, leading gently downhill, past school playing field on right. Reaching a minor road (Foxhill Lane), turn right and just after first property on left, turn left into narrow lane (Row Lane) for some 30 yards, then turn right into bridleway. Follow track along field edge, pass cottage on left, to emerge at road near Dunsden Green. Here turn right for a few paces, before turning left over stile, along field-edge with ditch on right. In corner of field bear right over footbridge to reach gravel drive of Chapman's Farm.

1 Cross drive and go straight across grass to find footbridge/stile in boundary hedge. Now turn left along hedged track (Tagg Lane) which climbs gently for a distance to pass solitary house close by on right. Continue ahead on drive until just after it bends left, then turn right over footbridge into field. Shortly pass right of tree-fringed depression and continue along mid-field line towards distant red-brick cottages, reaching road just to left of the pair. Cross into gravel track opposite and follow this past a pond (on right) and past barn (Comp Farm) and then ahead along edge of large field, with hedge on right.

2 In the next field, continue along right-hand side, passing two mature oaks, then, with field opening ahead, bear left and continue (still in same field) along field-edge, with hedge on right. At end of field pass behind pair of cottages and turn right along road for nearly ½ mile to crossroads.

Follow the signpost to Chalkhouse Green

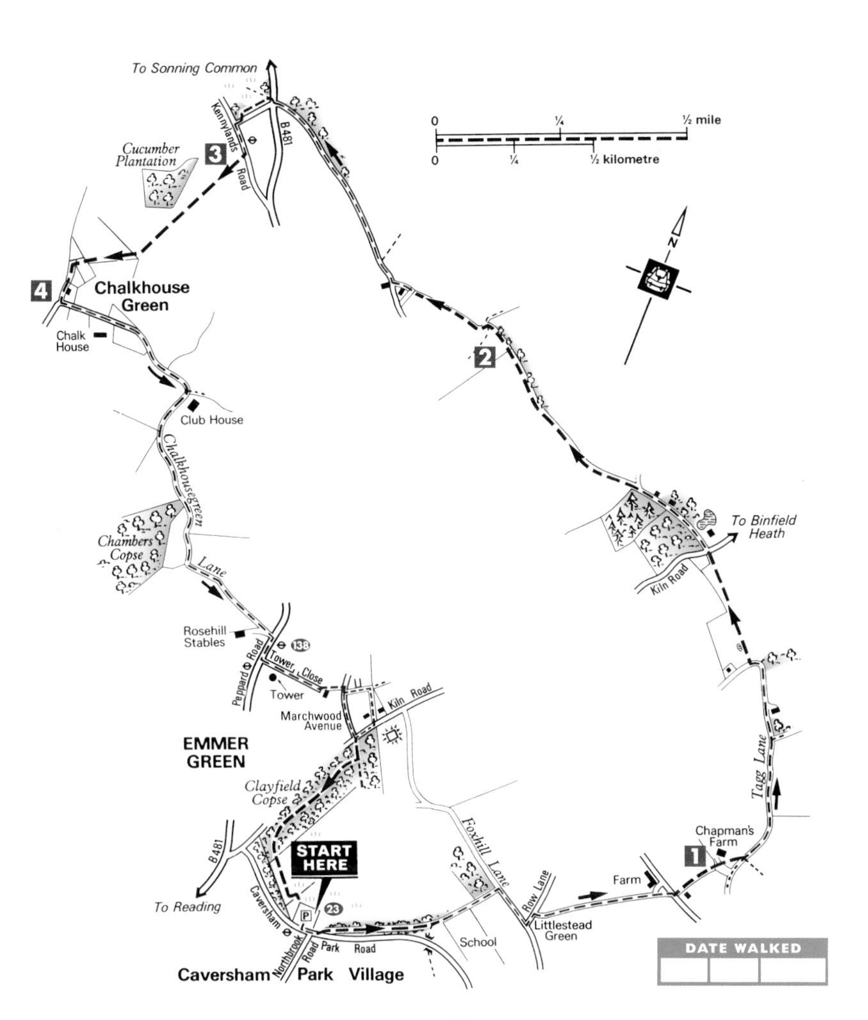

Carefully cross road (B481) and pass through metal swing-gate into Sonning Common's Millennium Green. Take left-hand perimeter path and look for wicket-gate on left, shortly before first corner of field. Turn right along lane for a few yards, then left along Kennylands Road.

3 Keep to verge on left for just over 100 yards, then cross road to stile by barrier and head across middle of large field in direction of distant buildings. On far side, bear slightly right over stile and follow wire fence through paddock. Cross stiles either side of small field ahead, then bear left alongside fence. After final stile go along gravel drive to reach road at Chalkhouse Green.

4 Now turn left and at end of tarmac surface enter hedged track (Chalkhousegreen Lane), then follow this winding, undulating bridleway for about ¾ mile. At road (B481) with care cross over and turn right for a few yards, then turn left into Tower Close, passing Emmer Green Tower on right. Pass to left of No. 15 and turn right along Marchwood Avenue. At road junction (Kiln Road) cross straight over into Clayfield Copse nature reserve. At end of wooden rails turn right and follow gravel path on right. Reaching a crossing path, turn left and shortly continue ahead across sports field, passing to right of pavillion, to return to car park at start.

Highland Wood and Walk Shaw

This mainly level walk explores the quiet woods and fields surrounding the tiny hamlets of Tinker's Green and Cane End, unspoilt countryside of the Chiltern Hills, today protected as an Area of Outstanding Natural beauty.

Distance: 4 miles
OS Map: Explorer 159 Reading
Start: Limited verge parking in lane on east side of former Fox Inn, Cane End (Grid ref: 680 795). For patrons, the Pack Horse on A4074 (Grid ref: 692 781) is an alternative.

With your back to the main road (A4074) and the Fox Inn on left, go ahead along lane, shortly to turn right at crossroads, now keeping to verge on right. Immediately after second property 'Owlswood' on right, enter field through gap in hedge and go half-left across small field to stile, then through middle of large field, aiming for gap to right of trees on far boundary. Maintain same direction across next field to row of seven trees – aiming for right-hand side of second tree from left. At this tree turn half-left to reach stile in hedge at road, just beyond power-line pole. Now turn right along road to bend, here, by 'Ashfield', turn right into hedged and fenced bridleway, eventually to enter woodland – Highland Wood.

1 Follow winding woodland path (waymarked with white arrows), running close to fields on left, finally descending quite steeply towards road. Just before reaching road, turn left along path through woodland strip (parallel to road) with field on left.

Bridleway alongside Chalkpit Shaw

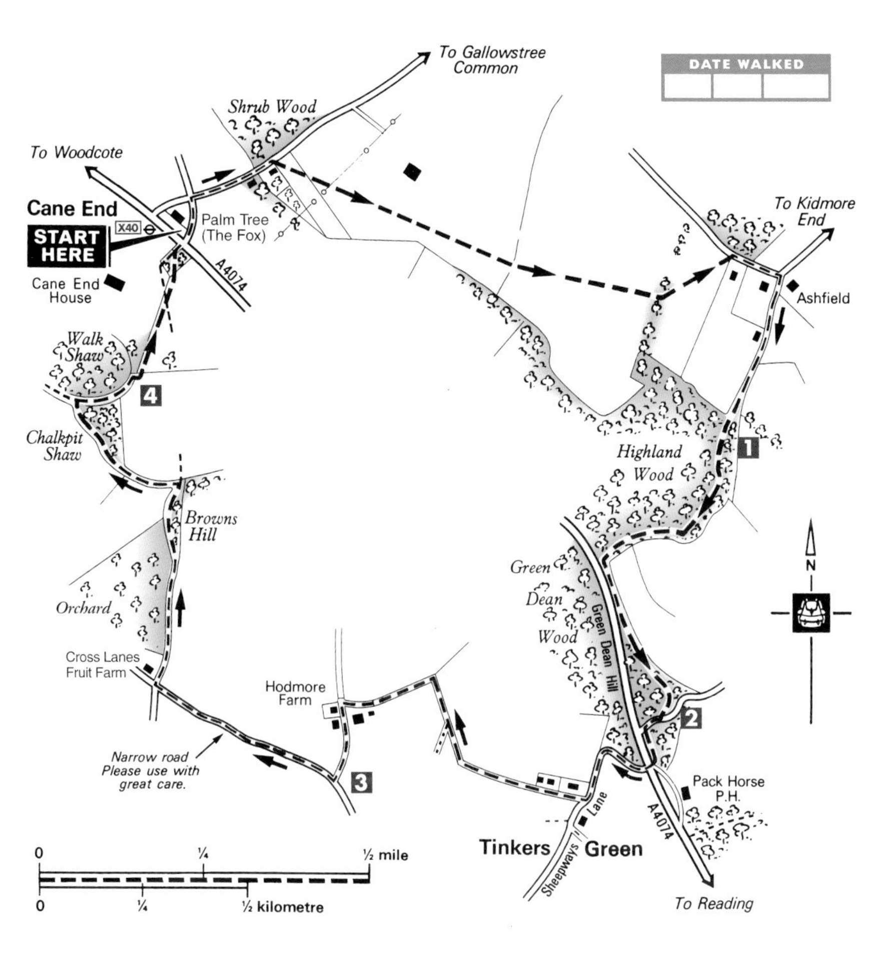

2 Reaching single-track lane turn right and climb (Green Dean Hill) to main road. Here turn left along verge for about 70 yards (within sight of the Pack Horse) and then with care turn right across road into lane opposite.

Follow lane through left-hand bend and at grass triangle, Tinker's Green, turn right along tarmac bridleway. Reaching thatched Hodmore House go straight on along path in wooded strip. Follow this path through right-hand bend and then, at end of trees, turn left on firm track, leading to buildings of Hodmore Farm. Here, in front of red brick cottage, turn left along concrete farm drive.

3 At road ahead turn right, keeping to right-hand side (facing oncoming traffic) until, immediately before property 'Cross Lanes' on right, turn right into hedged path. At bottom of descent (Browns Hill) follow path through left-hand bend, then climb steadily to reach a T-junction of tracks. Here turn right, following low bank of Walk Shaw on left.

4 Shortly our route swings out onto edge of field on right for just a few yards before turning left through gap, then follows beech hedge on left. At end of headland path, cross paddock ahead via two metal swing-gates and follow path through trees to reach another swing-gate by an entrance. Carefully cross road to return to start.

Nuney Green and Path Hill

This circular walk is largely through the sparsely populated, typical Chiltern beech woods around Collins End. A feature of the walk is the picturesque group of almshouses at Goring Heath, built in 1724 by a one-time Lord Mayor of London.

Distance: 4 miles
OS Map: Explorer 159 Reading
Start: Limited verge parking opposite former 'King Charles's Head' (Grid ref: 664 788) or near cross road at Goring Heath (Point 3).

Facing gables and ornate lattice windows of former pub, turn left along verge for about 150 yards, then turn sharp right into winding waymarked path (painted white arrows) for about half a mile through Gutteridge's Wood. On reaching narrow tarmac lane, fork left along it, soon leading to T-junction by 'Cross Ways' at Nuney Green.

1 Now turn left along gravel track until, with a thatched cottage either side, go straight on into narrow, holly-hedged path to enter woodland ahead. Soon pass right of pond and continue ahead, with long narrow field nearby on right. After end of this field carry on through wood until, some 20 yards beyond corner of large field nearby on right, fork left along waymarked woodland path for about 120 yards, then take right fork, soon with low boundary bank nearby on left. Disregard crossing paths and follow waymarked route. Soon, with field ahead, follow path along edge of woods, passing right of single-storey property before crossing road (Deadman's Lane) into footpath opposite.

2 After stile shortly ahead continue along fenced section to bridle-gate and, still beside fence on left, through a second gate. Now bear half-right across paddock to stile in corner where path continues between tall hedges to a another stile and on along grass track to emerge between buildings of Alnutts Hospital. Here turn left along roadway in front of this delightfully tucked-away group of almshouses, complete with Georgian chapel, clock and cupola. At entrance ahead to 'Chaplaincy', fork right along broad grass strip (permitted path) leading to wooden swing-gate by road junction at Goring Heath.

3 Pass to right of former Post Office opposite to enter tree-lined path, then at end of first field on right, turn right

Picnic at Path Hill

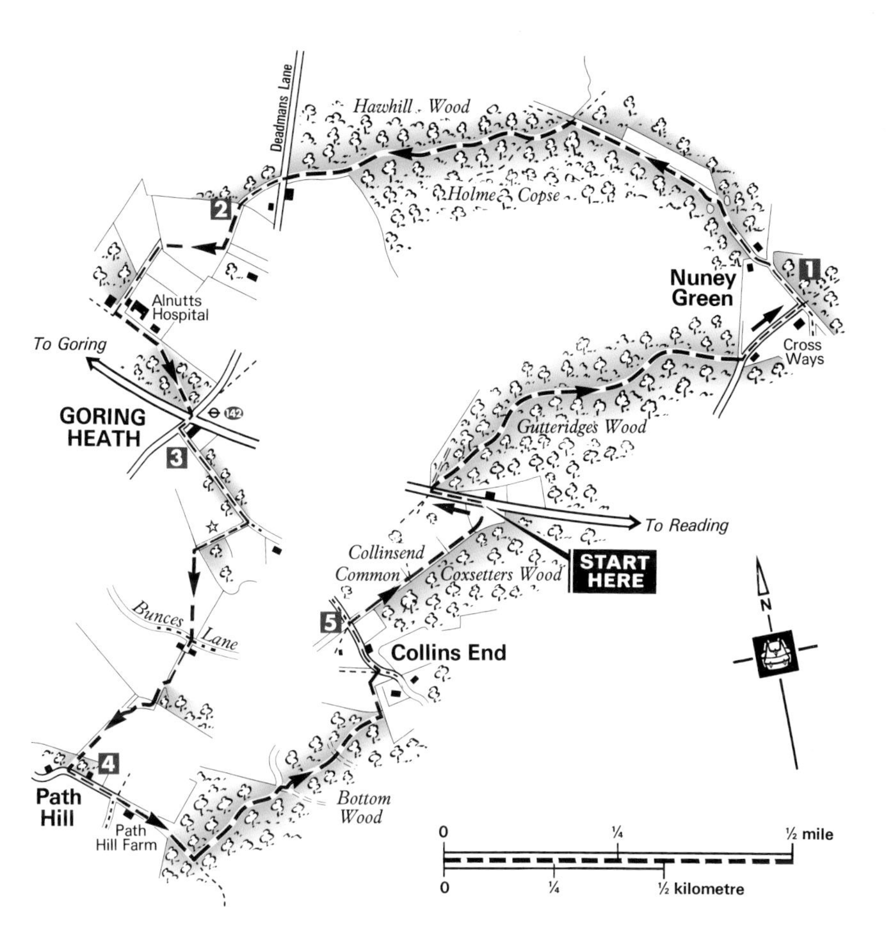

into very narrow fenced path.* At end of hedge on left cross stile and bear half-left across field towards left-hand of two distant cottages. Leave field over stile by gate and cross (Bunces Lane) to pass between cottages opposite. After field-gate follow hedge on right, then cross stile in corner and continue, now beside copse on left. After further stile go on down steep slope with fence nearby on left. Then bear left to follow steep path ahead, on either side of valley, then on through trees to emerge at corner of narrow lane at Path Hill.

4 Turn left along lane and go straight on, passing to left of Path Hill Farm buildings, into woodland ahead. Shortly, at bottom of small depression, turn left on descending woodland track. At bottom of valley, by field corner on left, bear right, up straight, climbing, waymarked woodland path. On arriving at edge of woods on high ground, (facing garden ahead) turn left over stile and up edge of field with hedge on right to reach, after another stile, road at Collinsend Common.

5 Now turn left along road and some 75 yards beyond Briar Cottage turn right along fenced track. Continue in field ahead with hedge on right and after two more stiles, go across middle of small paddock to stile in hedge, to return to start.

** In 1994 we complained to the Highway Authority that the path was too narrow. In 2009 it still is! So be careful but if you are injured or tear your clothes on the unnecessary barbed wire, do not let this go unreported.*

DATE WALKED

RAMBLE 6

Whitchurch Hill and Boze Down

This fairly energetic walk climbs up through the old village of Whitchurch to Whitchurch Hill, passes through typical Chiltern farmland, increasingly pasture, with some fine views across the Thames Valley.

Distance: 5 miles
OS Map: Explorer 159 Reading
Start: Small car park (free on Sundays) Pangbourne side of Whitchurch toll-bridge. (Grid ref: 636 767)

From car park, turn right over toll-bridge (pedestrians free), then turn left into private drive (a public footpath) towards the Mill. After some 75 yards turn right into narrow walled path leading to the attractive flint-faced Parish Church of St Mary the Virgin. At lych-gate bear right along tarmac drive to rejoin road and turn left along footway leading up through the picturesque village of Whitchurch. At top of village street bear left along narrower road, then shortly make use of the full length of raised verge on right, before crossing road to War Memorial opposite.

1 Keep along verge for about another 50 yards, then fork left up gravel path for a similar distance, then keep left to pass through swing-gate ahead, to follow edge of long field with hedge on left. At end of field, go through metal swing-gate into fenced grass track ahead. This passes to right of (almost hidden) Beech Farm buildings. Keep alongside hedge to cross concrete drive and enter paddock, following fence on left. DO NOT leave field through gate ahead but instead turn right, along edge of paddock. After swing-gate in corner, continue ahead along concrete drive to road. With care cross over and turn right, to pass St John's Church, Whitchurch Hill.

2 At end of churchyard, fork left across middle of green to enter, to right of houses ahead, a gravel drive. After terrace of cottages *(built 1901 to house workers of nearby Bozedown House)*, pass through old swing-gate, alongside extended curtilage and half left through middle of field towards left-hand end of distant row of trees. Leave field at kissing gate in hedge and turn right along farm track. After copse shortly on

Alpacas at Boze Down

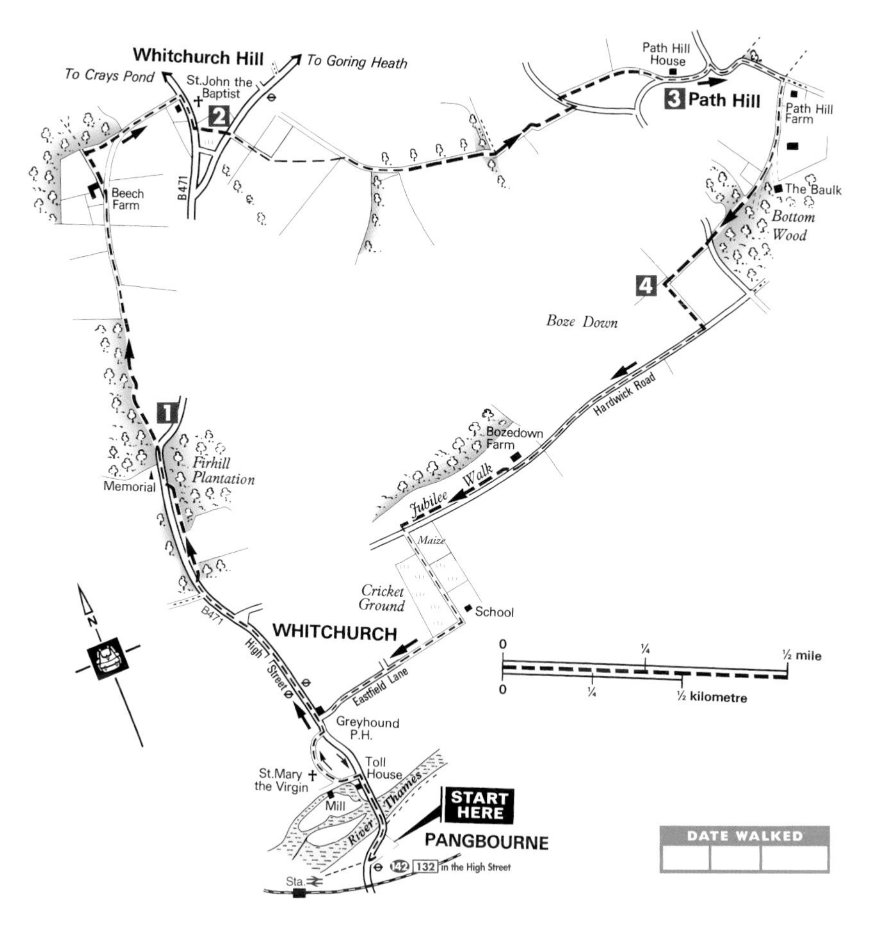

right, continue ahead with trees on left and splendid wide views to horizon on right. The right of way bears left of copse soon ahead and follows the twisting right-hand field edge, down to corner. Here turn left up track for some 70 yards, then turn right over stile and along left side of meadow to enter fenced path at corner.

3 Follow drive past cottages on left and continue up, alongside road past Path Hill House on left. Where road turns left, go right along winding lane. Facing yard of Path Hill Farm ahead, turn right along drive (public footpath) and where this bears left to a property, go straight on along wide path between hedges leading shortly to stileway on right, where path descends, increasingly steeply, through woodland. Emerging at road, cross to stile opposite and continue ahead along side of field with hedge on left, towards Boze Down.

4 In corner of field, pass through metal swing-gate. On reaching field just ahead, turn left and follow hedge on left down to road at bottom. Turn right along road (Hardwick Road), keeping if possible to verge on right. After The Old Farmhouse join raised path on right – Jubilee Walk – until about 75 yards beyond Whitchurch-on-Thames sign, turn left down bank and cross road to enter gravel track. *Hopefully you will have time to visit the Thyme Maze immediately on left*. At end of this track turn right along road (Eastfield Lane) to rejoin village street at the Greyhound pub. Here turn left to cross the River Thames again, leading back to car park at start.

Pangbourne College and River Pang

This circular walk to the west and south of Pangbourne follows the River Thames for almost a mile, then after climbing up to Pangbourne College (its woods a sea of bluebells in early May), descends through farmland to Tidmarsh before returning along the banks of the River Pang. (The College is the setting for the Falkland Islands' Memorial Chapel – open to the public every day from 9 to 5 pm.)

Distance: 5 miles
OS Map: Explorer 159 Reading
Start: Car park in centre of Pangbourne, next to Copper Inn (Grid ref: 634 765). Also easily accessed from station.

From car park, turn left along main road under railway arch. Continue along Shooter's Hill (A329), passing the Swan, eventually to follow footway on right with River Thames nearby, flowing sweetly! *Notice the ornate Edwardian houses facing the river (though some a little shabby now), dubbed locally when built as the 'seven deadly sins'!*

1 Where river starts to curve away from road, turn left across road and pass under railway, then immediately take left fork to join steadily climbing, winding, woodland path. Nearing the top, path touches edge of wood beside field, then continues through a more open area known as Berrys Copse. Keep near fringe of mature trees on left, looking out for metal swing-gate between two of them. From this gate bear left along field-edge with hedge on left. At end of field, maintain same direction through middle of next field, towards gap in mature trees.

2 Enter next field at corner of copse and immediately bear left along grass path, with hedge on left. At end of field with care turn left and follow road until reaching a T-junction. Here bear slightly right, into narrow lane opposite, leading to Pangbourne College – *founded in 1917, to educate and train boys for the Royal and Merchant Navies. In 1998 the College became co-educational.*

3 Go ahead, passing tennis courts on right and at crossing tarmac drive turn left. Go some 100 yards beyond

The River Pang

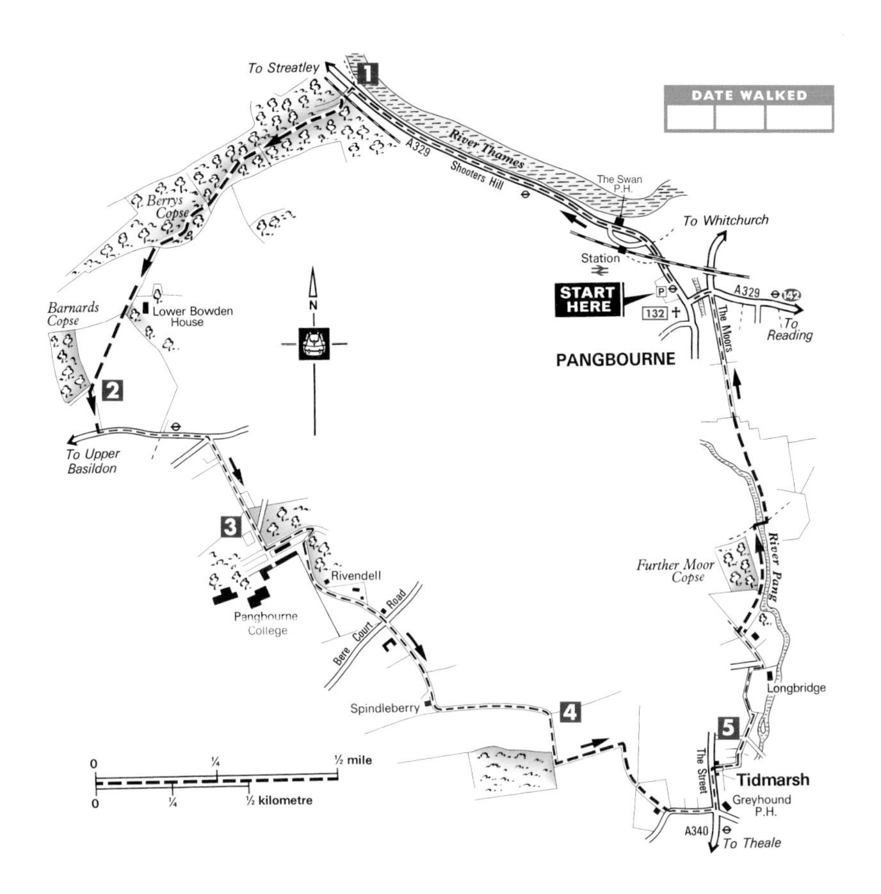

school building (dated 1991), turn sharp right on drive, then keep left down towards a field gate. Go ahead into tree-lined gravel track, gently descending, passing 'Rivendell' on left. After crossing road ahead (Bere Court Road), continue down gravel drive opposite until, at isolated house 'Spindleberry', enter hedged path and follow this through left-hand bend.

4 Eventually the path turns right and follows hedge on left along short end of field. Follow this grassy track as it continues in next field, with trees on right, turning sharp right at one point. At end of this field continue ahead through gateway, as path follows side of smaller field to swing-gate on corner of road by remains of Tidmarsh Farm. Now turn left along road to junction ahead, opposite the Greyhound.

Turn left along footway of The Street (A340) until, just after Strachey Close, turn right across road, into enclosed path.

5 Follow the fenced path, soon around a property called Longbridge. At entrance to this property, turn left along drive until, at junction of footpaths ahead, turn right through swing gate and along right-hand side of field to reach, after a stile and another gate, west bank of the Pang. Follow winding path beside the stream, to cross it at concrete bridge and continue beside it on the other bank. Where river bends left, keep straight on to enter broad tree-lined path at wooden swing-gate ahead. Eventually, continue along gravel road between houses, The Moors, leading to Reading Road. Here turn left to return to car park at start.

Moor Copse and Sulham Woods

This delightful walk, immediately to the west of Reading, is through the open farmland and steep woods around the old village of Sulham, providing some fine views across the Pang Valley, much of it within an Area of Outstanding Natural Beauty.

Distance: 3¼ miles
OS Map: Explorer 159 Reading
Start: Small parking area at entrance to Sulham Wood. (Grid ref: 648 745)

With your back to road, enter Sulham Wood via kissing gate on left. We use only the public footpaths so ignore any permitted paths. Follow most prominent woodland footpath until, after it bears right as the trees thin out, turn left at first path junction. Follow it down through trees, becoming increasingly steep. Emerging from woodland go through swing-gate and follow edge of field ahead with fence on left. At end of field on left, turn left over stile into narrow fenced path, with properties below on right. Reaching field ahead, go straight on along grass headland, with hedge on left, leading to road. Here cross over if you wish to visit the small but impressive church of St Nicholas, Sulham – built in the 1800s. It replaces a church that had stood hereabouts since the late 13th century.

1 To continue the walk, turn right down the road and about 40 yards after road junction, cross stile on left and bear slightly right through middle of field. After two stiles at footbridge, maintain same direction through next field to another stile in far corner. Now continue along edge of next field to follow on right, stream and Moor Copse.

2 Keep beside stream (passing right of power-line poles) to reach footbridge

Emerging from Sulham Woods

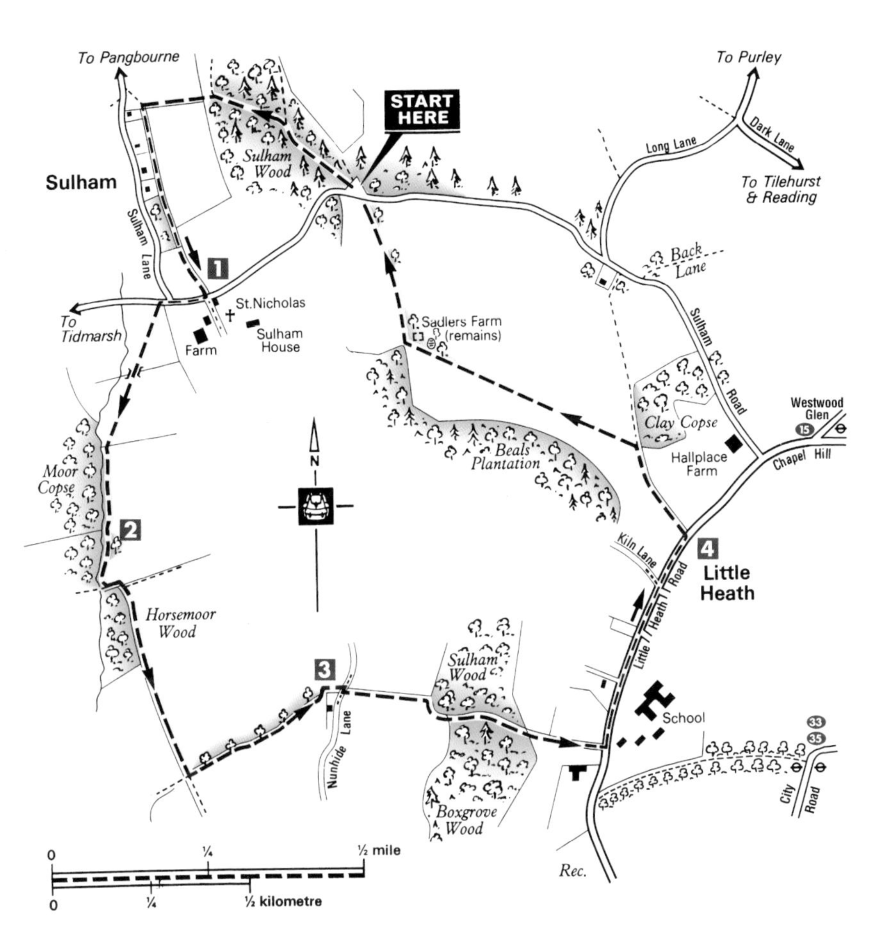

on right. Here *turn left* for about 50 yards, then turn right over stile and along field edge, with woodland (Horsemoor Wood) on right. Continue along headland of this large field with hedge on right, until turning left onto headland path, along right-hand side of splendid row of cross-field trees. *Standing on high ground away to right here are the remains of a red-brick tower – a folly built by the Rev. John Wilder, vicar of Sulham for 56 years until 1892. During this period he also rebuilt the church and Sulham House.*

3 On reaching gravel farm track at top of field (Nunhide Lane), step to the right a few paces, then continue ahead, up broad grass headland with hedge on left, to reach again the Forestry Commission's Sulham Wood. Now take care to turn right for some 30 yards before entering woods, then head steeply up narrow woodland path, eventually reaching metal kissing gate and a short length of enclosed path leading to road (Little Heath Road). Here, opposite school, turn left along footway for nearly ½ mile.

4 Where road bends right cross over outside No. 27 to stile, and follow edge of field with hedge on right. Where path soon divides, turn half-left on well-defined line which keeps to left side of large open field ahead. Just after pond by remains of Sadlers Farm, turn right along mid-field track, leading back to parking place at start.

DATE WALKED

North Street and Englefield Estate

This level, circular walk, is to the west of Theale, a village restored to tranquillity by construction of the M4. Our route is over fields and along quiet lanes, forming part of the extensive, visitor-friendly Englefield Estate.

Distance: 4 miles
OS Map: Explorer 159 Reading
Start: Car park (free on Sundays) at east end of Theale High Street. (Grid ref: 646 715)

Leaving car park, turn left along road and at end of houses on left, turn left into fenced and hedged path. After bridge over stream, turn left along old track at first, soon joining a gravel path through public open space, leading to road (Blossom Lane). Here turn right along lane until, at end of tarmac, turn left in front of Blossomend Cottage and pass beside metal field-gate along broad hedged grass path.

1 Reaching edge of golf course go straight ahead keeping a watchful eye on those teeing off from left or right. Follow pairs of way-marked posts, finally leading to swing-gate on far side of course. Here turn right along fenced tarmac path. Stately Englefield House and the spire of Englefield Church (to be visited later) may be seen in the distance on left. At road ahead turn right, to pass through the hamlet of North Street.

2 About 50 yards after last house (The Grange) on left, turn left over stile, to cross middle of field, soon following field boundary of hedge on left. After kissing gate at end of field turn left along road. At junction with main road (A340) carefully cross over and continue ahead along road (The Street) through Englefield – a picturesque village entirely in the ownership of the Englefield Estate.

3 At far end of village, turn right up drive past the Deer Park on left, to visit the impressive flint-faced parish church of St Mark's – *its earliest part is the nave, dating from 1190. Further up, among trees on left, stands Englefield House – a magnificent Elizabethan mansion (yes, she dined here in 1601), home of the Benyon family for over 250 years. The 7-acre gardens are open to the public every Monday, and Tue-Thurs in the summer. The estate covers some 14,000 acres comprising the Home Farm of 2,000 acres, twenty-three 'let' farms and 3,000 acres of woodland.*

There is now a choice of route. Recently the Estate kindly designated the main drive as a 'permitted path' for walkers, so you are free to follow the drive down to the handsome gatehouse (built in 1862). Skip text to point 4.

For a slightly longer alternative, retrace your steps through the village,

The tea shop and village stores

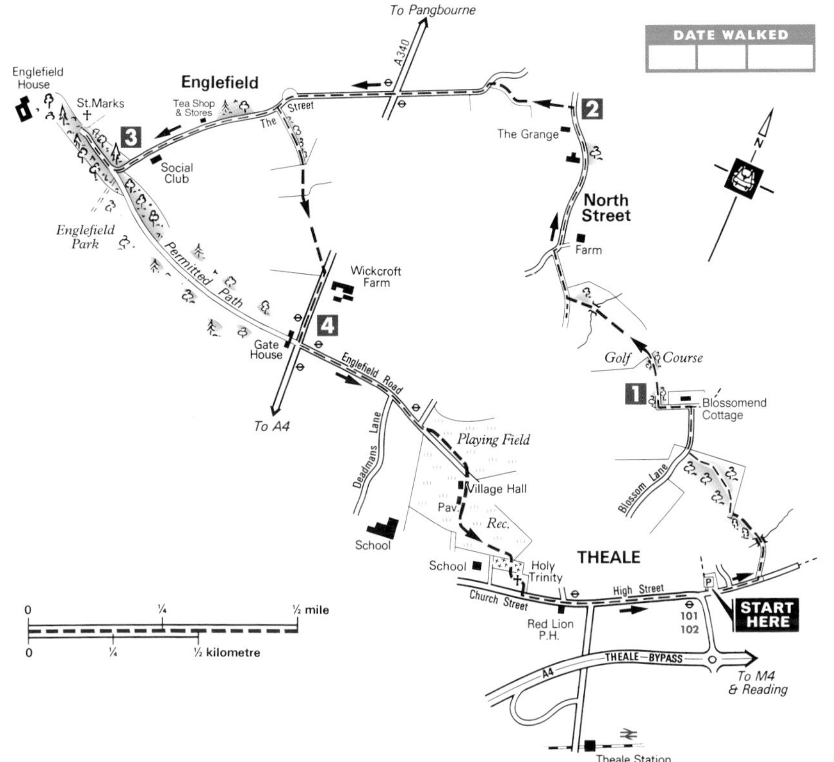

then immediately before last house on right, turn right through metal swing-gate and along fenced path through trees. At stile, cross field ahead to footbridge and ditch. From here bear slightly left over next field towards buildings of Wickcroft Farm, reaching main road (A340) after stile. With care turn right along road, keeping to verge on right, as far as Englefield Park entrance.

4 From gatehouse cross over into Englefield Road until, shortly beyond side road on left, pass through swing-gate on left to follow right-hand edge of playing-field, before rejoining road at second gate. Within a few yards cross road into Village Hall car park and head across playing-field towards church, to enter churchyard behind childrens' play-area. Follow path through churchyard, with the lofty Holy Trinity church on left, then beneath the tower. At road ahead, turn left along footway through Theale to return to start.

St Mark's Church

Kiln Pond and Simms Copse

This circular walk passes through the quiet, undulating countryside of fields and woods around Mortimer West End and is entirely in the county of Hampshire.

Distance: 4 miles
OS Map: Explorer 159 Reading
Start: Playing-field car park off Church Road, Mortimer West End. (Grid ref: 634 640)

From car park entrance cross road and turn left along footway. Soon look out for bus-stop and here turn right along woodland path (Benyon's Wood). Wide path descends and crosses gulley, followed by wooden walkway. Keep left at minor fork and cross single-plank bridge. Path rises steeply through pine trees, then widens, now with field close on left. Follow track as it turns right, away from field, and at next junction turn left, now descending to join gravel track leading to raised path across Simms Pond.

1 About 70 paces beyond pond turn sharp left on prominent track, soon climbing steadily, to pass Little Heath, just before reaching road. Here turn right, carefully, towards traffic until, at start of woodland on left, cross road into path descending steeply (Heathland Copse). Cross gulley and from stile into field aim slightly left, dipping down to stile between holly trees just beyond field gate.

2 After stile, turn right, down to nearby junction, then turn left. At a point where track ahead starts to bear left (and just beneath overhead cables) look for path turning sharp right and follow this through trees to stile into paddock. Now keep close to hedgerow bearing left, to cross two stiles with track between.

3 Continue ahead to a another pair of stiles and after second of these two,

Our path through Simms Copse

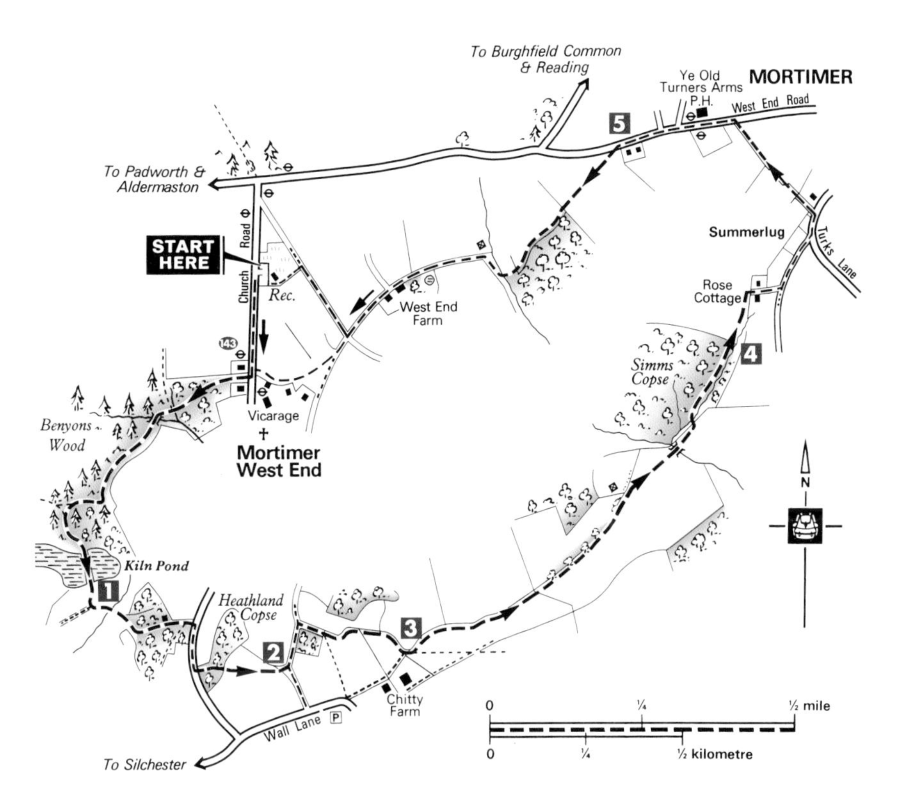

turn left and follow hedge on left. At bottom of this large field, cross stile ahead and keep to right side of mature trees until, with power-lines overhead, path heads on mid-field line towards stile slightly left of white house on hill-side ahead. Cross footbridge over brook and after about 100 yards ahead look for stile in left-hand fence, just beyond two large oaks. Now follow steadily climbing path up through Simms Copse.

4 Towards top of copse path leads to stile into field corner. Follow right-hand field edge to leave beside house shortly ahead (Rose Cottage). Follow drive and turn left along lane just ahead. Where this joins a road (Turks Lane) continue to the first house on left, 'Bosket', to turn left beside it. After stile ahead, path follows edge of field then passes through gap in hedge into adjoining field and with hedge now on left, continues to reach road at footbridge. Here cross over, turning left, to pass or visit – the Turner's Arms.

5 Prepare to cross back over road when opposite last house on left – Travellers Cottage – and turn left beside it for a few paces before bearing right on cross-field farm track, towards right-hand end of trees on far side. Keep on this track as it runs down beside the copse. At bottom of descent turn right along track and follow this, keeping left past West End Farm. At junction of ways (where metalled-surface starts) those returning to car park should turn sharp right. Then at end of first (unfenced) field on left pass through swing-gate and turn left along side of playing-field to return to start.

Walkers returning to the bus stop should continue ahead for a few yards to the footpath forking right, which leads to the road.

DATE WALKED

Ufton Court and Seward's Gully

This delightful circular walk passes through a variety of Berkshire's countryside, visiting a spectacular Elizabethan manor house in its parkland setting and the diminutive medieval church at Sulhamstead Abbots.

Distance: 4 miles
OS Map: Explorer 159 Reading
Start: Limited verge parking near crossroads about ¼ mile southwest of Sulhamstead Abbots. (Grid ref: 644 677) or from the western edge of Burfield Common (see map)

From crossroads, go south along Hollybush Lane for nearly ½ mile, keeping to verge as far as possible, until reaching row of light-painted houses. Opposite no. 78 turn right along drive towards Benhams Farm. Pass between farm buildings to enter fenced path ahead, soon continuing along wooded strip with field on left. Reaching broad gravel drive go straight on and turn right along lane (Island Farm Road). At end of field on left, enter corner of woodland, known as Poors Allotments.

1 Now gravel extraction has finally been completed here, we can follow the definitive line of the footpath once more. So follow diagonal line, crossing several new culverts to reach stile on far side. From corner of field keep straight ahead, beside hedge on left, leading to a high stile in next corner.

2 Pass between cottages and along their drive, then cross over (Camp Road) and continue ahead along edge of broad ride (Church Plantation) to road on far side. Bear right for a few yards to road junction, turn left through gateway and bear right into field through kissing gate. Go half right across field to another gate on far boundary. Here turn right along edge of grass, shortly to view on left the stunning Elizabethan front of Ufton Court. *This late 15th century house, was once the home of the Perkins family, Catholic recusants who gave sanctuary to many priests in the days of Elizabeth I.*

3 Now turn right along tarmac drive between broad avenue of oaks and

Ufton Court ~ ***Also visited via a different route in the first series***

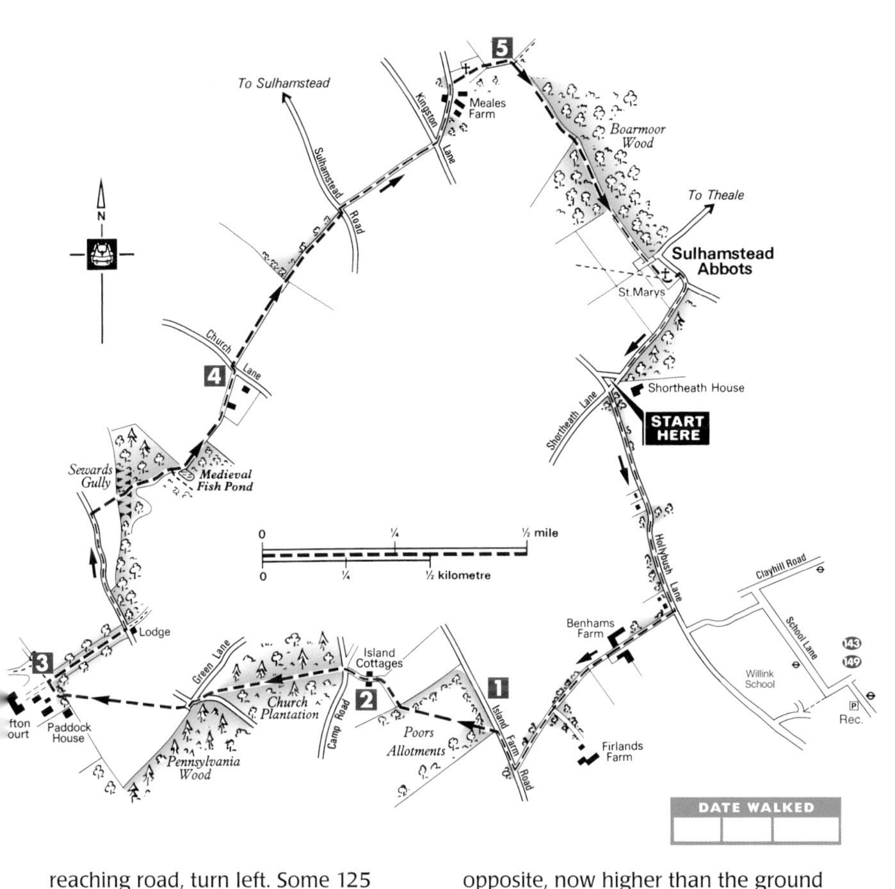

reaching road, turn left. Some 125 yards beyond end of woodland on right, turn right through gap at signpost and head very slightly left down across field into trees. Path descends to cross small footbridge over Seward's Gully, then climbs to stile and carries on along edge of woodland. Look right along here for tower and spire of St Peter's Church, Ufton Nervet; keep an eye open for deer in this area. Keep left of pond (a medieval fish pond, one of several in this area) and go straight on, soon on right-hand side of field, to enter track past Bowling Alley Cottage.

4 At road (Church Lane) turn left for some 20 yards, then right over stile to follow edge of two fields, the first now fenced (report as too narrow) the second with scattering of oaks on left, and distant views towards a stately pile, Englefield House. Emerging from corner of field, cross road into gravel track opposite, now higher than the ground either side, due to gravel extraction. At road junction cross into St Michael's Lane ahead. After buildings of Meales Farm, turn right through metal swing-gate into St Michael's burial ground – *all that remains of the Church (built in 1912 and demolished in 1967) is the porch, left as a shelter for funeral mourners.*

5 Leaving far end of burial ground by stile, go ahead on field edge to path junction in field corner and turn right over stile and follow left side of field, down to old gateway at bottom. Keep straight on over stream and climb steeply up woodland path. Near top of climb continue ahead along edge of woodland with fields on right. After parking area, path ahead crosses churchyard of 13th century St Mary's, Sulhamstead Abbotts. Just beyond Church Cottage, turn right along road (Short Heath Lane) to return to start.

Ufton Green and Padworth House

This walk follows the restored Kennet & Avon Canal and also provides fine views over the wide Kennet Valley. It is particularly suitable for those using public transport as it can be a linear walk from Theale train station or the bus-stop at Wigmore Lane; or a circular walk from Aldermaston. For motorists, the car park at Tyle Mill Bridge offers yet another starting point.

Distance: Linear: 4 miles (Wigmore Lane) or 5½ miles (Theale). Circular: 6 mile (plus 2 miles if starting from Wigmore Lane).
OS Map: Explorer 159 Reading

1. From THEALE TRAIN STATION – turn left along road and on far side of canal swing-bridge turn right along towpath for just over 1½ miles to reach Tyle Mill Bridge.
2. From BUS STOP on A4 – go to south end of Wigmore Lane, cross railway and turn right, then left through copse. Shortly, after footbridge, turn right along bank of River Kennet. Follow this to cross bridge/weir, then swing-bridge shortly ahead. Now turn right along towpath for about ½ mile to Tyle Mill Bridge.
3. From ALDERMASTON TRAIN STATION – from platform 2 cross car park and road to turn left beside Kennet & Avon Canal. Cross main road (A340) and follow towpath, switching to south bank at second road bridge (Ufton Bridge). After about two miles this circular walk joins the linear routes (just beyond lock) at Tyle Mill Bridge.
4. From TYLE MILL BRIDGE (car park nearby – Grid ref: 627 692).

1 For all four walks, turn away from Tyle Mill Bridge and go south along road until, at end of property 'Rose Court' on right, turn right into narrow path beside fence and pass over two stiles and then along bottom edge of first field to stile.

DATE WALKED

To Pangbourne
THEALE
To M4 & Reading
To Theale
A4
102
Theale Station
2 START HERE
1 START HERE
4 START HERE
Wigmore Lane
Swing-bridge
Canal
To Sheffield Bottom
Sulhamstead Lock
Swing-bridge
Tyle Mill Bridge and Lock
Folly Farm
Church (remains)
Ufton Green

Continue on same line now through a plantation of young trees. After further stile path starts to bear left slightly until, after another stile by metal fence it climbs half-left to reach and follow top edge of field, with tall hedgerow on left. After swing-gate and remains of chapel on left, reach another gate at road (Church Lane), at lower end of Ufton Green.

2 Now keep straight on across grass, then along road. Shortly, at end of first field on right, turn right over stile. Follow short length of fence on right and maintain same direction across middle of field. Then continue ahead alongside next two fields. At end of copse (Linley Shaw), bear right, down wide track then immediately left round bottom edge of field, to footbridge in corner. Maintain same direction through middle of next field to opening in field boundary ahead. From this point take a slightly diagonal line towards trees on right, leading into a hedged grassy track. Follow this track to emerge at road and turn left. Just past bungalow at Lodge Farm, pass over stile on right and follow right-hand side of parkland, climbing slowly up towards Padworth House (rebuilt 1769 – since 1963 a Sixth Form International College).

3 At top of field pass through wooden swing-gate and along path through woodland strip past lake then across drive, to metal swing-gate in front of St John the Baptist church (dating almost entirely from 1130).

'I welcome each new visitor as I did the one before;
For centuries I've waited here for you to cross my door.'

4 Facing lych-gate turn left for about 60 yards and continue down drive. Bear left of The Bothy, then turn right, round barn on right. After stile just ahead go down field to stile by gate at bottom. Now bear slightly left to footbridge in far left corner. Continue ahead across middle of two more fields to join path twisting and turning across bridges, passing Padworth Mill. Shortly bear left into wide gravel track (Mill Lane) and at end of this, cross canal. For Aldermaston Station and bus-stop on A4 go left along minor road over railway. To return to Tyle Mill Bridge, Wigmore Lane or Theale station, follow canal bank – see map.

Kennet and Avon Canal

Roman Amphitheatre and Foudry Brook

This unusual walk, through the peaceful rolling fields to the south of Mortimer, with extensive views over Hampshire, reaches its climax at the extraordinary remains of the first century Roman amphitheatre at Silchester.

Distance: 5 miles
OS Map: Explorer 159 Reading
Start: Village Car Park opposite Horse & Groom Public House, Mortimer. (Grid ref: 655 646)

Facing pub, turn right along Victoria Road, keep left into West End Road, then take first left into unmade road (St John's Road). After about 40 yards turn right into another hedged, unmade road. Follow this track (a public footpath) crossing two other roads until, at far end, turn right along tarmac surface of Drury Lane. Shortly, at junction, turn left into Turks Lane, soon cross county boundary into Hampshire (notice bench-mark). Where road forks, keep right (Simms Farm Lane) and where tarmac stops, go straight on along gravel drive to pass buildings of Simms Farm. Continue ahead down sunken track and where this divides keep right, down slope, to bridge over stream (West End Brook). Ignore path following fence to right but instead bear slightly left across middle of narrow field to find footbridge into woodland ahead – Nine Acre Copse.

1 Climb path straight ahead through copse to far side of wood. Bear slightly left across middle of field and after some 125 yards notice midfield crossing path (reinstated after pressure by the RA) and continue ahead to stile at field boundary. From here go ahead, down increasingly steep field to find footbridge over ditch in trees. Now bear slightly left uphill to reach squeeze-stile into sunken lane on far side of field. Turning right up track soon leads to corner of road with entrance gate to Roman amphitheatre close by on right.

Silchester's 12th-century church of St Mary, the timber-framed manor house

A Palm Sunday service in the Roman Amphitheatre

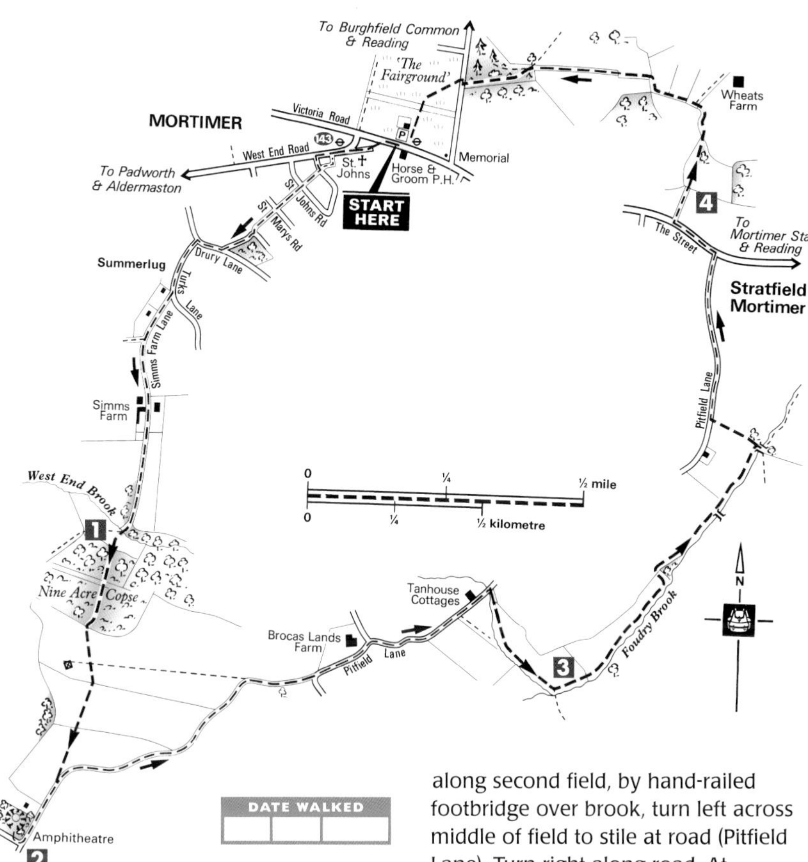

and the remarkable Roman town walls are just a few yards ahead.

2 Now retrace your steps, staying on the sunken track, weaving its way, finally to join road (Pitfield Lane), soon reaching Brocas Lands Farm. Here fork right, towards the distant spire of St Mary's Church, Stratfield Mortimer. Just after Tanhouse Cottages on left and immediately beyond bridge over stream, turn right into hedged path to kissing gate and follow right-hand side of field beside stream. At corner of field, facing gate, turn left to follow, below on right, Foudry Brook.

3 Continue along right-hand side of next long riverside meadow, finally leaving by stile in corner. Pass left of copse, now along edge of field with brook still on right. About half-way along second field, by hand-railed footbridge over brook, turn left across middle of field to stile at road (Pitfield Lane). Turn right along road. At junction turn left (The Street) and shortly at bend, immediately after 'Alvernia', turn right down gravel drive.

4 After stile at end, climb left side of field to stile at top and then follow hedge on left, leading to pair of gates at path junction. Here continue ahead on path through paddocks, beside metal railings. In corner of third paddock path turns right for about 50 yards, then turns left into next field, with fence and trees on left. Shortly enter fenced path with trees now on right. At end of field turn left into copse and after about 60 yards fork left, leading to road. Here, go a few yards right to enter through metal swing-gate an area known as the Fairground. Now go half-left, crossing railed heathland strip, to another metal gate, then keep left of tennis courts, to return to car park at start.

Grazeley Church and Hopkiln Farm

Is this the land that developers forgot? How can it be so peaceful and feel so isolated when it is actually so close to the motorway? There is not too much of it, so take your time and enjoy it – while you may.

Distance: 3¾ miles
OS Map: Explorer 159 Reading
Start: Limited verge parking in Fuller's Lane, off Grazeley Green Road (Grid ref: 688 676)

With verge on left, start off along winding Fuller's Lane, past Grazeley Manor Farm on left. Go under railway and about 200 yards after bridge, opposite Poundgreen Farm, turn right into Pump Lane. About 80 yards beyond drive to Hawthorn Cottages on right, turn left over plank-bridge and head along field edge, with ditch on left and the area known as Lambwoodhill Common on right.

1 At waymark post, continue on field-edge path, still beside ditch. Reaching metal gate ahead, at corner of field, cross stile into roadway (Church Lane). Shortly, turn left through wooden swing-gate into corner of churchyard of Grazeley's small flint-faced Holy Trinity Church.

Keep to right-hand side of churchyard, then head across middle of field towards left-hand end of distant buildings (Gravelly Bridge Farm). Leave field across footbridge, and go left along road a few paces to stile opposite. Cross over and after length of green metal fencing follow surfaced track, then right-hand side of narrow field to stile by gateway in corner. From this point continue ahead on left side of next three fields – a surprisingly peaceful stretch of old tree-dotted parkland. Look out for deer!

2 At end of third field, go through gateway into narrow lane by Hopkiln Farm and turn right (Kybes Lane). Follow it round left-hand bend (beside Foudry Brook on right) until, just

Near Hopkiln Farm – countryside that developers have so far overlooked!

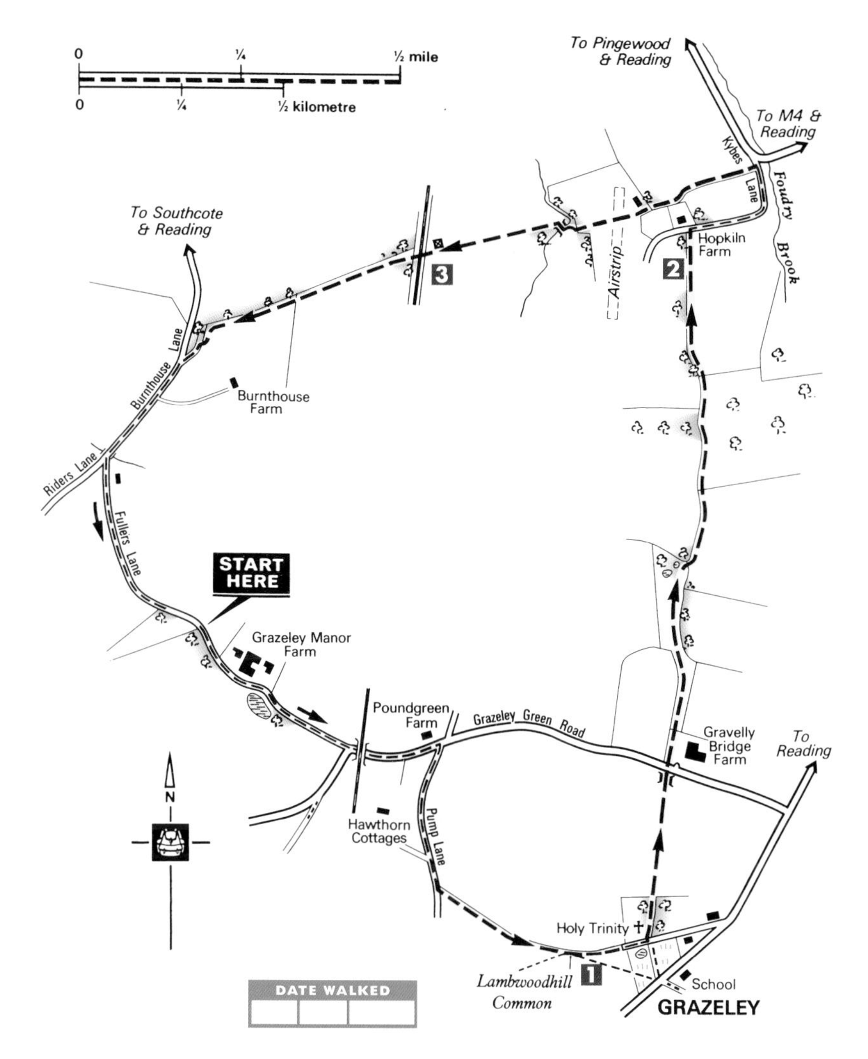

before road junction ahead, turn left beside gateway and along broad grass field-edge strip. Leave field at small stile in corner, pass through gap in hedge, and keep left of building on right. Then bear slightly right over occasional air-strip, to ditch and bank to right of kink in far field boundary. Just ahead, in next field, turn right over footbridge. This remote, seemingly unnamed little brook was chosen to form the division between east (Wokingham) and West Berkshire. Now bear left across middle of field, passing just left of distant pylon.

3 With care cross railway ahead (Reading–Basingstoke line) using stiles both sides, then continue along broad grass strip with fence on right. In next field notice waymark post pointing left, across corner of field to stile and footbridge in hedgerow, (or stay on field-edge to reach same point). At road shortly ahead the heavily-fenced establishment on the right is the Royal Ordnance factory, Burghfield. Now keep left along road (Burnthouse Lane), then at bridge over brook (Burnthouse Bridge) bear left into Fuller's Lane to return to parking place at start.

Devil's Highway and Beech Hill

This interesting walk passes through an area of gently rolling farmland to the south and east of Stratfield Mortimer, about a quarter of which follows the ancient Devil's Highway.

Distance: 5¾ miles
OS Map: Explorer 159 Reading
Start: Lay-by just NE of Stratfield Mortimer. (Grid ref: 676 646) Alternative start St. Marys Church. (Or station)

From lay-by, with care, continue along road towards Stratfield Mortimer, then immediately after entrance to sewage works turn right, up edge of field with hedge on right. Near top of field bear left across corner of field to reach and turn left along road (Mortimer Lane). At road junction, with care cross over, turning left, then after about 50 yards turn right into gravel drive, towards the impressive tall stone church of St Mary's. Bear left of church lych-gate, cross brick bridge to gap ahead, then turn right and follow raised field-edge path, soon along bank of Foudry Brook.

1 At end of field on left, with footbridge on right, turn half-left through middle of field to pass through tunnel under railway. After footbridge path passes right of large tree and pond, via a second footbridge then continues to right-hand corner where field narrows to join hedged track, leading after left and right bends, to road at metal barrier. Turn right along this quiet lane until just after buildings of Butlers Lands Farm, turn left into broad hedged track – the Devil's Highway – the Roman road from London to Silchester.

2 Follow this ancient highway for about 1½ miles (marking the county boundary) the surface has been much improved in recent years, following pressure from the Ramblers' Association. Eventually reaching solitary red-brick cottage, turn left along road for some distance: a peaceful, winding hedged lane with wide verges, suggesting an old drove road. Look out for a white railed bridge at bend in

Enjoying good views towards Stratfield Mortimer

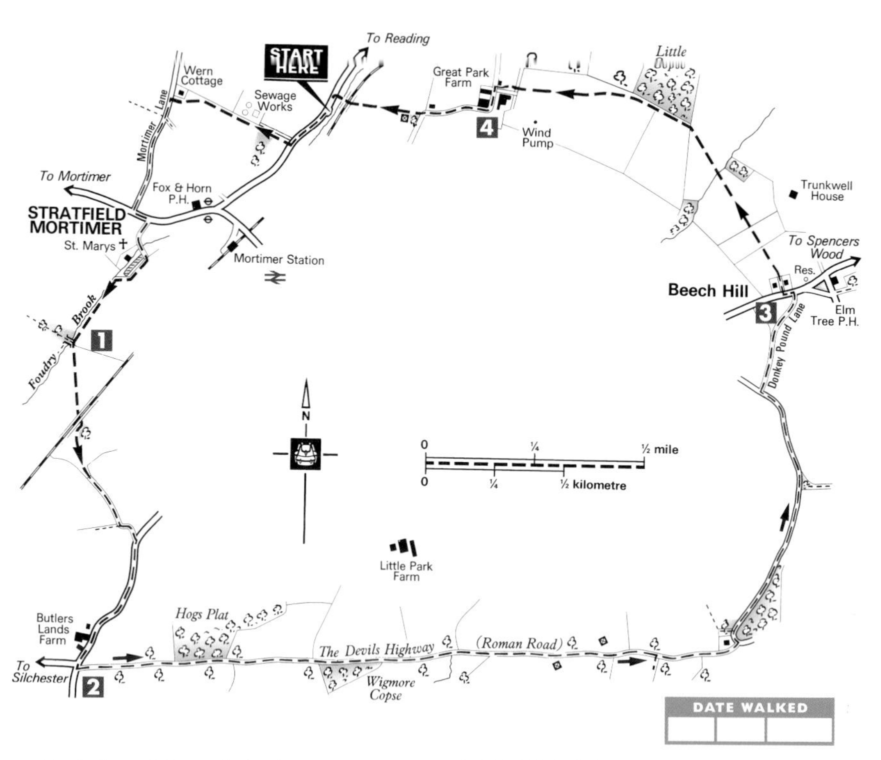

road, then 100 yards further on turn right into gently climbing restricted byway – known as Donkey Pound Lane. Continue on gravel track past houses to road ahead. Here turn left to continue walk, but turn right for about 30 yards to visit the water reservoir given to the residents of Beech Hill in 1897 to mark "sixty glorious years" of Queen Victoria's reign.

3 Retracing your steps, continue along road for about 60 yards, then turn right up fenced path between cottages and after squeeze-stile keep straight on across middle of first field. After second squeezeway continue on same line through series of kissing gates to reach at top of climb, corner of woodland (Little Copse). Now follow field-edge with copse on right. Cross stile by field gate and, before end of woodland, definitive path bears slightly left away from fence line and heads towards right-hand side of Great Park Farm buildings ahead.

The large property in distance on right is Wokefield Park: originally an 18th century mansion, Queen Victoria once took tea in the garden. Owned by Alfred Palmer (of Huntley & Palmer) from 1900 until 1936, it then became an approved school and then, since 1987, a Conference and Training Centre.

After crossing stile on far side of this field, go ahead soon alongside farm buildings. At farm road (the main highway before railway was built in 1848) turn right and go ahead between barns and past delightful farmhouse on left which dates from the 16th century.

4 Soon after this house, farm road bears right. Continue along it until it turns left by pair of red-brick cottages. At this point, go straight ahead into field, keep 20 yards to right of nearby pylon and maintain same direction over brow of hill, down to stile in field boundary. With great care cross railway using stiles either side. After bridge over Foudry Brook just ahead, turn left along road to return to parking place at start.

Shinfield and Three Mile Cross

Dare we say it, but imminent re-development should improve this route through some disused agricultural research buildings. However, there is plenty of interest for the walker along these paths and through the fields.

Distance: 4¾ miles
OS Map: Explorer 159 Reading
Start: Free car park Shinfield village green. (Grid ref: 733 678)

With British Legion hall on left cross road (to new health centre) and join main footpath. Shortly, near top of slight rise, turn right into hedged path, leading to main road (A327). With care cross over, turn left, then right into Fairmead Road. At end of road turn left on unmade surface (Oatlands Road). Immediately opposite No. 37 turn right into narrow footpath between gardens and bear left over footbridge, now with fields on right. Emerging at road (Cutbush Lane) turn left, then take second turning left, Leyland Gardens.

1 At end of first garden on right, turn right and follow narrow footpath leading to main road (Hollow Lane). Carefully cross using steps both sides, then follow path ahead, before turning left along roadway then turn right, between old buildings of one-time National Food Research Institute, due soon for re-development.

2 Follow this roadway through left-hand bend until, facing old timber-framed building, turn right to enter and pass along right-hand side of churchyard of Shinfield's attractive brick and flint-faced parish church of St Mary (built 1170). At road (Church Lane) turn right for about 40 yards, then left into footpath and at corner of old cemetary turn right on metal path. Pass playground on right then continue on path between fields. At end of first field

Shinfield FP 13. A well-used route to Ryeish Green School

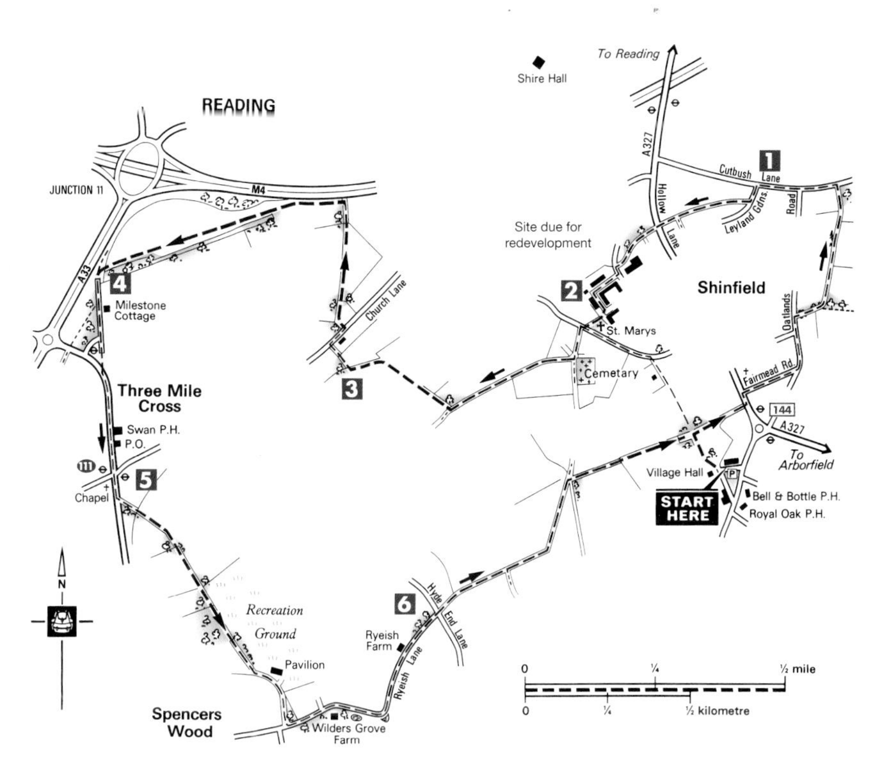

on right, turn right, at first with fence on right, then hedge, soon continuing down middle of open field, before turning left along field edge with hedge on right.

3 Just before power-line pole, turn right through gap in hedge, cross end of narrow field and after stile, go ahead to road (Church Lane). Now turn right for about 40 yards then cross over to stile and follow hedge on left-hand side of small field to find stile in corner.

Continue in next field, still with hedge on left. After stile and footbridge at end of field keep straight on until, facing the M4, turn left over stile. The right of way follows trees on right for a short distance. Then pass into next field on right, through wide gap in tree line. Follow hedgerow on left to gate at far end.

4 Go ahead, bearing left, into the old A33. Shortly, in front of first house, Milestone Cottage, note old milestone inscribed 'Southampton 43' etc. At end of cul-de-sac, keep straight on along main road through Three Mile Cross.

5 About 100 yards after crossing Church Lane, turn left into broad hedged path and after stile follow side of field beside hedge on right. After further stile continue along edge of fields ahead with hedge now on left, soon with playing field on other side of hedgerow trees. Eventually, emerging on drive (near pavilion) go ahead, to turn left along narrow winding road (Ryeish Lane.)

6 At road junction, keep straight on into gravel path between fields. Ignore footpath on right and at concrete farm track ahead cross over and bear right into broad grass track. Reaching open area, still follow hedge on left to complete the circuit, soon turning right towards buildings at start.

DATE WALKED

Swallowfield Park and Thatcher's Ford

This circular walk follows paths and tracks through peaceful countryside mainly in the historic parish of Swallowfield, close to the county boundary with Hampshire. Due to the low-lying nature of the area, it may be better enjoyed in dry conditions.

Distance: 4 or 6½ miles
OS Map: Explorer 159 Reading
Start: Riseley Memorial Hall car park, Odiham Road. (Grid ref: 723 630) To confirm parking availability for group walks tel: 0118 988 5444.

From left-hand exit of car park cross road, turning left, to enter through stileway footpath on right. (Trees along here conceal line of the Devil's Highway – the Roman road from London to Silchester.) At road ahead cross carefully into Sun Lane and follow this narrow hedged road past Coldharbour Cottage. Soon bear left along traffic-free Bull Lane, go under bypass, then turn right at T-junction until, outside farmhouse, turn right into hedged byway (Spring Lane).

1 Follow this old lane as it wanders through the countryside, with occasional far-ranging views on left towards Mortimer and Beech Hill. Just before bypass bridge can you spot, away to left between trees the Priory, one of Berkshire's most historic houses? At the end of Spring Lane (the old house here on the corner is Queen Anne's Mead) go straight on and shortly cross road, opposite 'Handpost', to turn left along footway, then turn right into quiet Charlton Lane. At first road junction (Trowes Lane) continue for some 40 yards, then turn left into gravel drive. Immediately before drive turns right, enter narrow fenced footpath, with ditch below on right. Stay on this path (ignoring one turning right), finally leading through two paddocks to reach road.

Refreshment available here ... on the longer route.

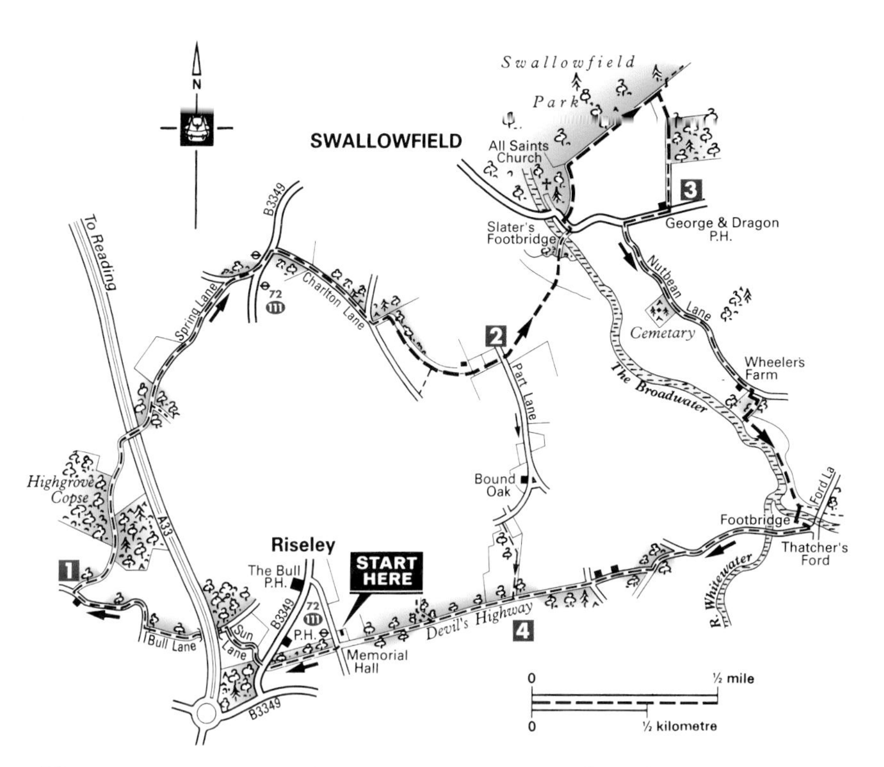

2 *For shorter route:* Turn right here (Part Lane) and follow this past assorted property until, by 'Bound Oak', bear right. Shortly, at junction with Trowes Lane, continue 40 yards ahead and turn left over stiles either end of farm building. Following hedge on left, maintain this direction through middle of field to meet and follow hedge on left again, then after stile in corner turn right to join longer route (skip text to point 4).

2 *To continue longer route:* Cross road (Part Lane) and follow field path through two fields, to reach footbridge over the Blackwater River, then continuing ahead between hedges, emerging at Salter's Bridge, in Church Lane. Cross over, turning left along footway. Unless wishing to visit All Saints' Church (built 1256) just ahead, turn right over stile before house and follow edge of large field, soon turning away from church, beside hedge on left. Just beyond handful of mid-field trees, turn right at finger post into newly-hedged, wide path. Pass right of copse where fenced path leads on to road at George & Dragon.

3 Here turn right, then first left into narrow Nutbean Lane. Continue past bend at Nutbean Farm and just beyond Wheeler's Farm, turn right over ditch, into footpath beside field. At next stile turn left and head through riverside meadow, passing confluence nearby of Rivers Blackwater and Whitewater. Just before field end (by Thatcher's Ford) turn right over river footbridge, then left across end of field to stile by gate, then turn right along road. At first fork keep left of grass triangle and follow this lane, round a twist at one point, soon passing Devil's Highway name-plate just before minor crossroad. The shorter route soon joins from a field on right.

4 Firm road surface disappears after white Banks Cottage and we continue ahead, straight on along line of one-time Roman road, back to Memorial Hall car park at start.

DATE WALKED

RAMBLE 18

Pudding Lane and Farley Hill

This circular walk is through the gently undulating farmland, woods and still peaceful countryside around Arborfield Cross and Farley Hill.

Distance: 4½ miles
OS Map: Explorer 159 Reading
Start: Free car park at Arborfield Cross, about 200 yards down Swallowfield Road from 'Bull at Arborfield'. (Grid ref: 760 670)

Leaving car park, turn right along road and shortly, at end of playing-field by barn, turn right into broad hedged track – Pudding Lane. At main road ahead (A327 Reading Road), turn left along footway. Shortly after SECOND bus-stop on left, turn left into Greensward Lane. Immediately after last house on right, turn right through stileway into Pound Copse. Fork left along Permitted Path and at end of copse turn right to cross stile and follow field-edge with hedge and trees on left. In next field, at junction of paths, turn left and continue on broad path with hedge on left.

1 At end of field turn right, with fence and young trees on left. In field corner, path continues on wide track through right- and left-hand bends, passing red-brick Kenneys Farm, and on to reach road (Swallowfield Road). Here turn right, keeping to verge on right. About 100 yards beyond Tanners Farmhouse turn left across road into broad climbing woodland track (Kiln Hill). Reaching top of slope carry on along the byway, soon continuing on road ahead to crossroads (Bunce's Shaw).

2 Go straight on along this quiet lane until some 50 yards after two red-brick houses and bridleway on left, turn left to stile at gap in roadside trees. Cross small field and pass left of large oak,

Springtime at Long Copse

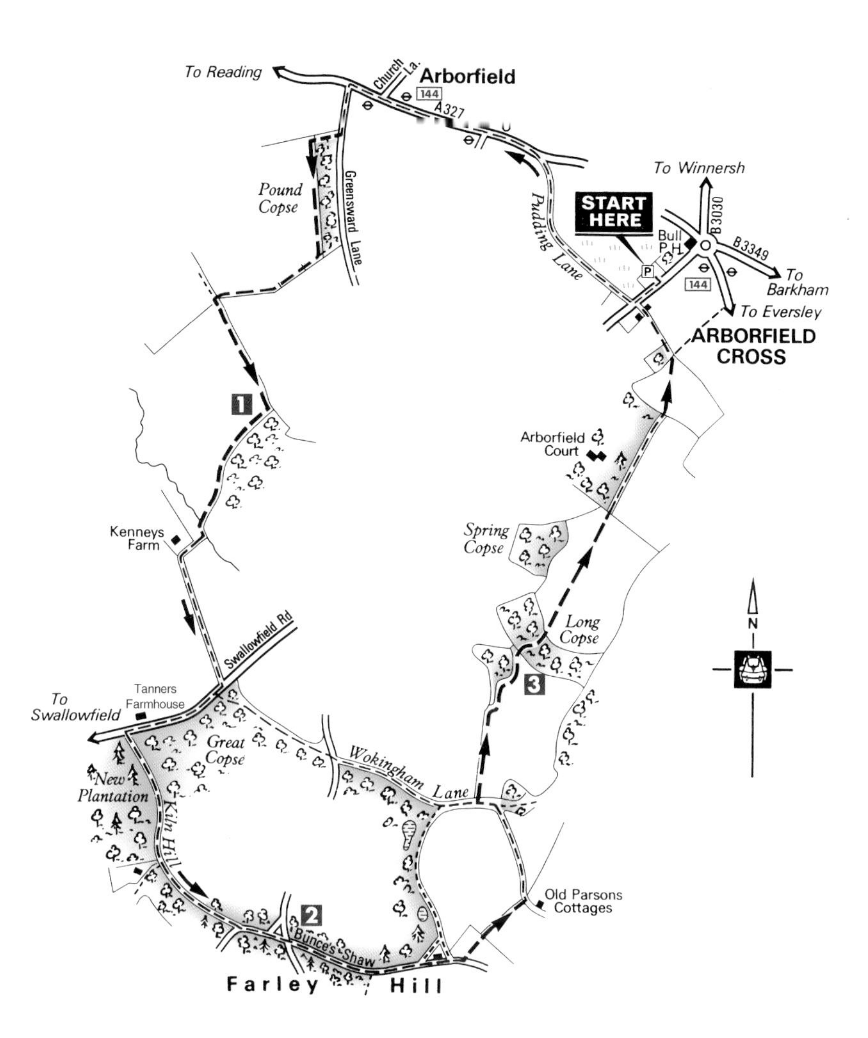

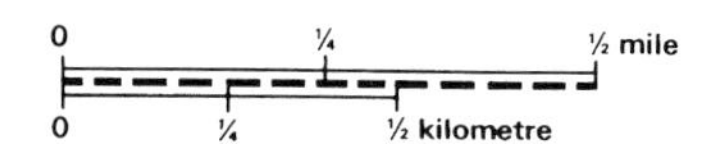

then straight on across open field to turn left along hedged track. At T-junction of tracks turn left for nearly 100 yards, then bear right to join field-edge path with hedge on left (and distant views towards Reading).

3 At woodland ahead bear right up bank and continue along winding field-edge to enter woodland strip at field corner. After two kissing gates keep straight on, now along top of ridge to reach gate at right-hand end of conifers on horizon. Continue along narrow fenced path beside high hedge of Arborfield Court on left. After next gate bear slightly left down through middle of field to another gate in far left corner. Turn left and after small footbridge and gate, follow edge of field with houses on right. Leave field in front of thatched cottage, shortly to turn right along road and back to car park at start.

DATE WALKED

Fleet Copse and Rectory Farm

This circular walk provides fine views over the gently rolling countryside around the old village of Finchampstead and includes some water meadows adjacent to the Blackwater River, the county boundary with Hampshire.

The optional extension around Longmoor Lake in California Country Park adds ½ mile to the distance.

Distance: 5 or 5½ miles
OS Map: Explorer 159 Reading
Start: Wokingham District Council's California Country Park. (Grid ref: 785 650)

From car park return to Country Park entrance; avoid traffic by using the minor path through trees on left of drive. Turn right along road keeping to footway, then at No. 63A 'The Cuckoos', carefully cross road and into a railed footpath beside wide gravel track. Cross the track where path continues beside timber-clad building on left. After kissing gate ahead continue straight on along fenced path with fields both sides. Along here look half-left to catch a glimpse of Finchampstead Church in trees on high ground, visited later on this walk.

1 At road (Commonfield Lane) at Beech Cottage, go straight on, up through three fields with gates between and hedge on left. After kissing gate at path junction turn sharp right between wooden rails, and follow this fenced path for nearly a mile, with fields and woods on both sides. Finally, reaching a stile, cross private drive, go ahead through swing-gate into a new plantation and follow wire fence on right. On far side, after two swing-gates, turn right along verge beside road (B3348).

2 About half-way down hill, turn left into gravel drive, beside Vann House. On reaching buildings of Fleethill Farm, keep straight on along wide fenced track beside Fleet Copse. At end of track, keep right and cross stile ahead beside gate. Hug left side of field, which forms part of the broad, flat valley of the Blackwater River.

3 Cross two stiles in far corner of this field and within a few yards turn left up broad woodland track (Longwater Lane). At start of houses, to continue walk turn left, but first go ahead for some 20 paces to post on left where a plaque gives details of an incident involving King Henry VII back in 1501. Retracing your steps, follow climbing path with fence on right to emerge at The Village (B3348). Here turn left along road, keeping to footway on right. Just after houses on right, turn right up tarmac drive towards Rectory Farm.

4 At gateway, just before buildings ahead, enter fenced path on right and, at end of field on right, turn right. Now follow this climbing fenced path through left and right turns. At a T-junction turn left up hedged track to reach, after swing-gate and several steps, on top of a man-made mound, the part-Saxon Parish Church of St James. Beyond the tower bear right down broad drive and just before the Queen's Oak turn left along White Horse Lane. *The section shortly ahead, between two bends, is part of the Devil's Highway – the Roman road between*

Beyond Beech Cottage

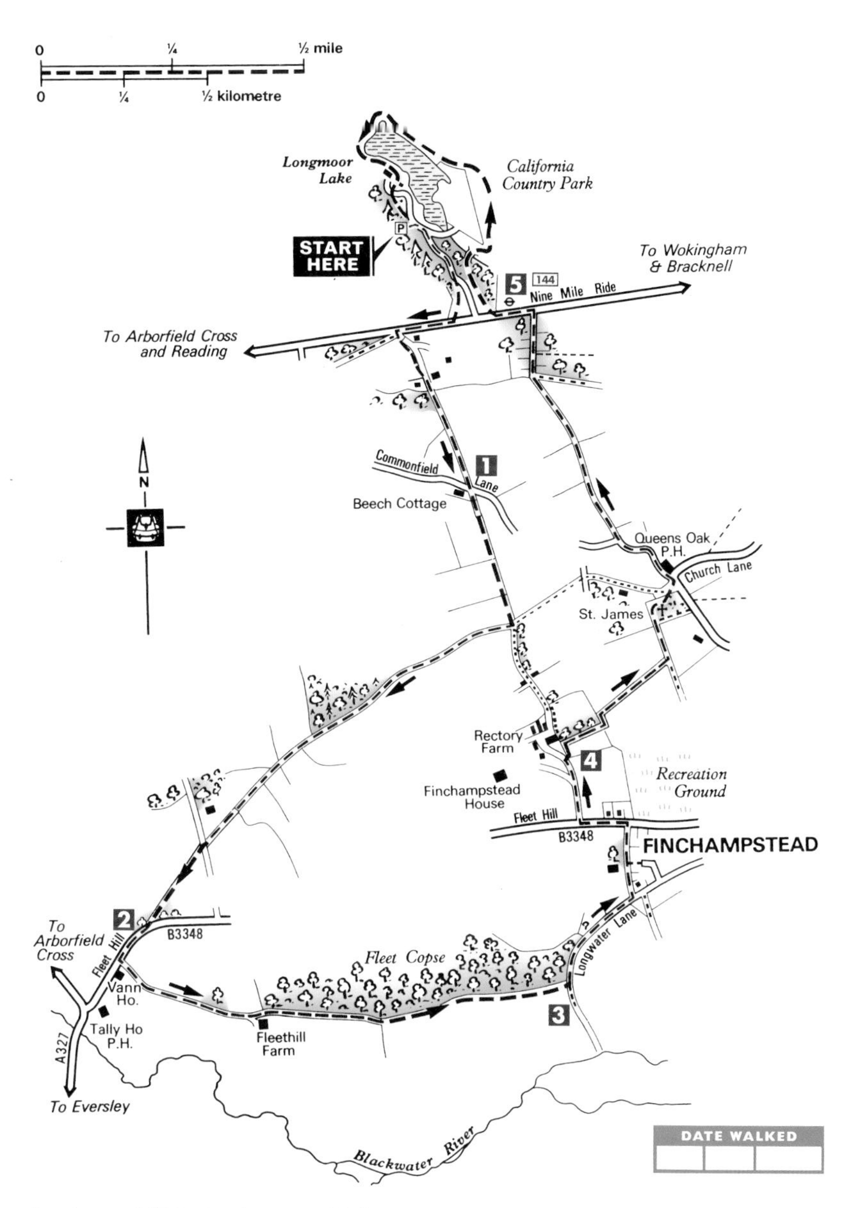

London and Silchester. At second left-hand bend, fork right through bridle-gate into descending fenced track. At houses bear left to join gravel drive (Warren Lane) and at road ahead (Nine Mile Ride) turn left along footway opposite.

5 At entrance to Country Park, enter narrow woodland path on right, running beside the drive. After about 150 yards, for the extended walk, bear right over a wooden footbridge and shortly turn right along raised path which curves to left. After passing open parkland with pond on right, path descends into trees soon with Longmoor Lake nearby on left. Continue around edge of lake, pass a picnic area, then after green-tiled building take short woodland path on right of drive to return to overflow car park at start.

Hatch Farm and Loaders Lane

This short circular walk explores a small corner of countryside, embracing fields and tracks around the fringe of Winnersh and the wider spaces of neighbouring Arborfield, starting and finishing on a fine open space at historic Sindlesham.

Distance: 2½ miles
OS Map: Explorer 159 Reading
Start: Car park on west side of Bearwood Recreation Ground, Sindlesham. (Grid ref: 776 698)

Facing road, leave car park in far left corner, carefully cross Mole Road (B3030) by roundabout and turn right into Mill Lane to follow winding footway. About 60 yards beyond the buildings of Hatch Farm on left, carefully cross road to stile opposite. Turn right along edge of two fields with fence and, shortly, M4 motorway on right. After footbridge, steps and stile, (originally built for Berkshire County Council by RA members in 1980) keep straight on along side of field ahead, with fence and M4 still on right.

1 About half-way along length of field, at signpost, turn half-left through middle of meadow to a stile near far corner. Continue on same line across corner of next field to leave it over stile and small footbridge. Now follow hedge along top of this small field before leaving by turning left over stile at corner into broad wooded track. Shortly ahead at bend, keep right along track, Loaders Lane.

2 Follow track, soon passing copse on left (Gravelpit Wood), until finally, by pair of grey-brick cottages, turn left into broad gravel track (Julkes Lane).

Opposite first property on right, Carters Hill Stables, turn left up bank onto cross-field path leading slightly left towards woodland. After footbridge and stile continue to end of woodland on left, then head slightly right across open field to stile. Keep straight on through two small paddocks and after two stiles in the corner, turn right along track.

"Keep straight on through two small paddocks..."

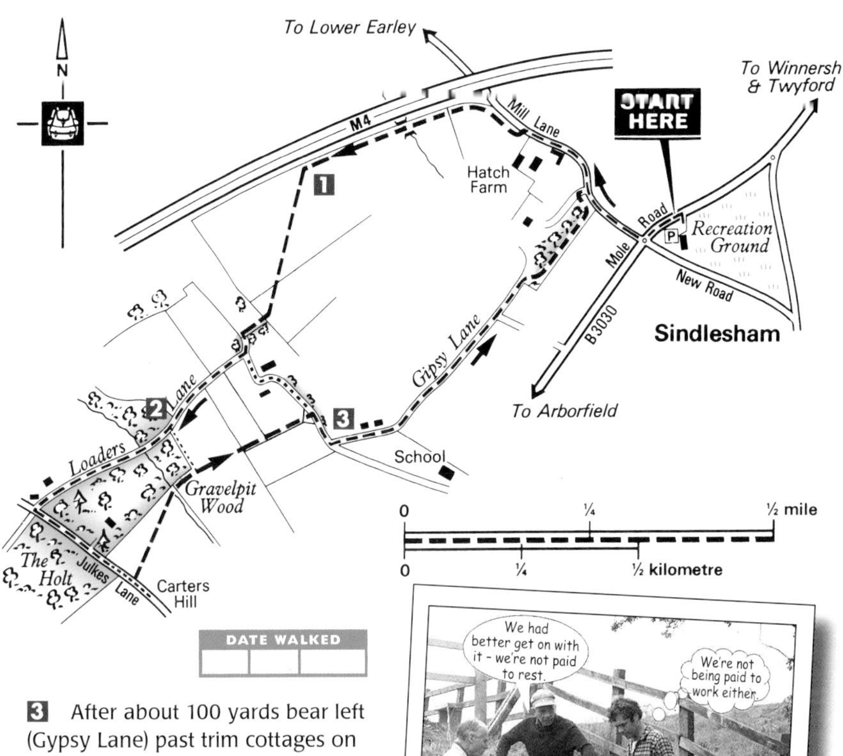

DATE WALKED

3 After about 100 yards bear left (Gypsy Lane) past trim cottages on left. Track narrows between hedges then widens again with new houses just visible on right. Where this track turns right, go straight on over shallow ditch and through stileway into narrower path beside club car park. Path now leads diagonally right through light woodland then bears left around head of pond, to join gravel drive at road. Here with care cross road to footway, turning right, and retrace your steps to car park at start.

April 1980. East Berks RA members take a well earned rest from erecting the footbridge near the (new) M4 in Winnersh.

Theale Lake and Whitehouse Green

A varied walk through fields and meadows, along lakesides and canal banks, within the still mainly rural parish of Burghfield. Easily accessible by bus from the fringe of Reading at Calcot, or starting from Burghfield village.

Distance: About 5¼ to 6 miles
OS Map: Explorer 159 Reading
Start: **1. Calcot**, Beansheaf bus-stop in Charrington Road. Grid ref: 663 716
2. Burghfield village green – roadside hard-standing. Grid ref: 666 685

1. From bus-stop take narrow tree-lined path leading to gate into park-land. Here bear slightly right towards left side of gap in trees, to cross wide culvert over ditch. Follow grass strip to wide wooden footbridge and turn right along bank of Holy Brook. At end of meadow turn left over two stiles with railway between. Go ahead through meadow to cross stile onto Hissey's Bridge, over River Kennet. Immediately after bridge turn right down slope and with stream close on right, follow surfaced path ahead. Pass under M4 and immediately turn left.

1 After 75 yards bear left to cross wooden footbridge and go straight on along wide track, with open views across Theale Lake – a popular sailing venue. At end of lake, facing metal gates, bear left into fenced grass path.

2 Eventually this uneven path turns away from motorway, leads to footbridge and turns sharp right along bank of deep ditch (Clayhill Brook). After sharp left turn path reaches stile at road. Cross road, turning left along verge for 40 yards, then turn right down steps to stile. Follow left side of two fields ahead, leading to Green Farm. Take track on left of farm buildings and continue along roadway. If returning to Burghfield village, take cross-field path on left, by Victorian farmhouse and cross two fields to reach School Road.

To continue the circular walk, after farmhouse look for gap into first field on right and skip next paragraph.

2. FROM BURGHFIELD, start from north side of hedged triangular green. With back to 'Six Bells' follow right-hand footway (past the Old Rectory – garden often open to public) and bear right at crossroads. At end of houses on left, turn right into School Road and where tarmac stops turn left over stile, bear half-right on cross-field line, passing left of power-line pole. After gap in hedge turn half-left up next field, aiming just left of single tree. Cross lane ahead via gaps in hedges, as you join the route from Calcot.

3 **For both routes** bear slightly left, down field, to cross wide sleeper-

Theale Lake

bridge. Here turn right, then left in field corner and climb field-edge with splendid row of oaks as your guide. After top of rise, bear right out of field, into enclosed strip. On reaching lane turn left, and where this turns right, bear left into field entrance and along edge of first field then, after plank bridge in corner, straight across next field to road (Theale Road).

4 Turn right along footway and at Bennett's Hill, cross over and take first turning left (Folly Lane). Follow this quiet lane until, at sharp left bend (Whitehouse Green) bear right into brick-flanked gateway and immediately bear left along boundary of 'Barnyards' for some 60 yards. Here turn left through archway in hedge, then right, along broad strip to stile. Maintain same direction on cross-field path ahead, and at bottom corner continue down track to gate at road. Now turn right and where road forks, bear left (Bottom Lane). Follow lane (or grassy strip along lakeside) and where lane turns left, turn right into woodland, along winding path, soon to cross low bank on left. Continue between stream on left and lake on right, shortly to reach towpath of Kennet & Avon Canal.

The canal section between Newbury and Reading, known as the Kennet Navigation, is the oldest of the three parts which make up the 'K & A', having opened in 1723. Along its 18½ miles, 20 locks were built to retain the water; it falls 134 feet between the two towns.

5 Turn right along canal bank for a little over a mile, passing Theale swing-bridge, Sheffield and Garston Locks, to reach M4 bridge.

Walkers starting from Calcot retrace their steps from here via Hissey's Bridge. Those starting from Burghfield turn right in front of M4 bridge and follow path towards Theale Lake (see second paragraph).

DATE WALKED		

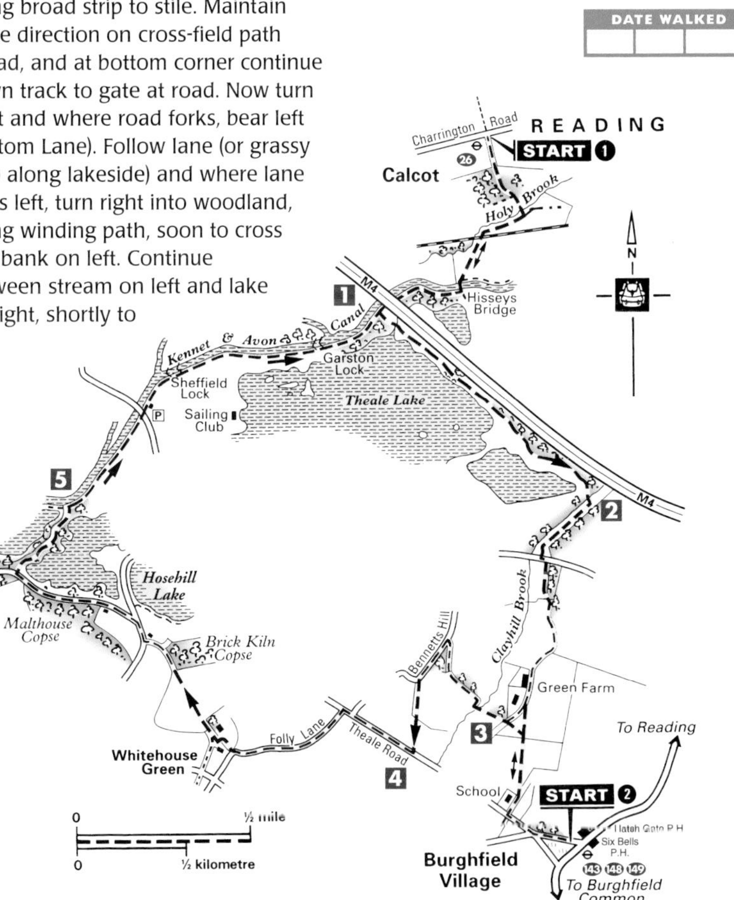

RAMBLE 22

Milkmaid's Bridge and Holy Brook

This easy stroll starts near the centre of Reading. The low-lying Kennet River meadows have kept the builders at bay, leaving a wedge of almost hidden countryside on the town's doorstep, known mainly to fishermen and wildlife.

Distance: 4 miles
Os Map: Explorer 159 Reading
Start: Bus-stop on bridge in Berkeley Avenue just west of Elgar Road traffic lights. (Grid ref: 714 726)

Note: Motorists can start from Reading Link Retail Park in Rose Kiln Lane – see map – beginning walk at last paragraph.

From lay-by at bus-stop cross over Berkeley Avenue, turning right. Then cross Lower Brook Street and immediately turn left down steps to bank of River Kennet. Here turn right under bridge and along riverside. *This part of the river forms a section of the Kennet & Avon Canal, opened in 1723, spanning the 18½ miles between Reading and Newbury. Parts of the canal follow the original course of the river while some stretches were specially built, to carry the 20,000 tons of goods being transported annually at the end of the 18th century.*

1 After nearly a mile along the towpath, pass under one modern road bridge (Rose Kiln Lane) and then shortly another (A33). Soon on the right, pass the distinctive modern Thames Water control building in Fobney Meadow, a design in metal and glass by prominent architect Nicholas Grimshaw. Reaching old pumping station buildings, turn left over bridge and then right, to pass Fobney Lock. Continue along broad gravel track, now on left bank of canal.

2 Here the Kennet parts company with the canal for a stretch but soon reunites where our route goes over an unusual 'labyrinth' weir and turns right along the bank. Pass under railway arch shortly ahead, continuing along riverbank to reach and turn right over white-railed footbridge. Go ahead to view the pleasantly situated Southcote Lock. *The Victorians built a pumping station here in 1850 to provide a much needed fresh-water supply for the fast-growing population of Reading.* From the lock retrace your steps a few yards and cross the narrow iron-railed footbridge – Milkmaid's Bridge – then bear right along the drive, away from the lock.

3 Go under railway, turn right and follow path at foot of embankment. Then turn right again under railway and immediately left, up narrow rising

Brookmill Bridge

path, soon between railings. Cross footbridge over dismantled railway to emerge at Wensley Road. Turn left and shortly, just beyond North Lodge Mews, left again, up tarmac path to follow track alongside Courage Park at first then leading to road by entrance lodges (Coley Park). Here go straight on, through swing-gate, to reach Wensley Road again. Now turn right and shortly cross over to bear left into The Old Lane (a public footpath). Pass through a gate across the footway and reaching road junction bear right along Brookmill.

4 Just beyond Brookmill go ahead over bridge across Holy Brook. (By turning right here, a delightful detour is possible through this unspoilt river scenery – see map.) To continue our circuit, however, turn left after bridge and follow bank with stream on left. Eventually this leaves the water-meadow area and leads on, with what might be called the 'hanging gardens of Coley' on the opposite bank.

5 At end of parking area, cross stream over broad footbridge, left again for a few paces, then turn right across a courtyard leading to footway through distinctive modern development, Admirals Court and leading-out onto Rose Kiln Lane. Continue ahead, using traffic island to cross over then turn right at traffic lights, back into Berkeley Avenue.

** Reputed to be the only crossing point in the country where a road meets a street, a lane and an avenue. Not a lot of people know that!*

DATE WALKED		

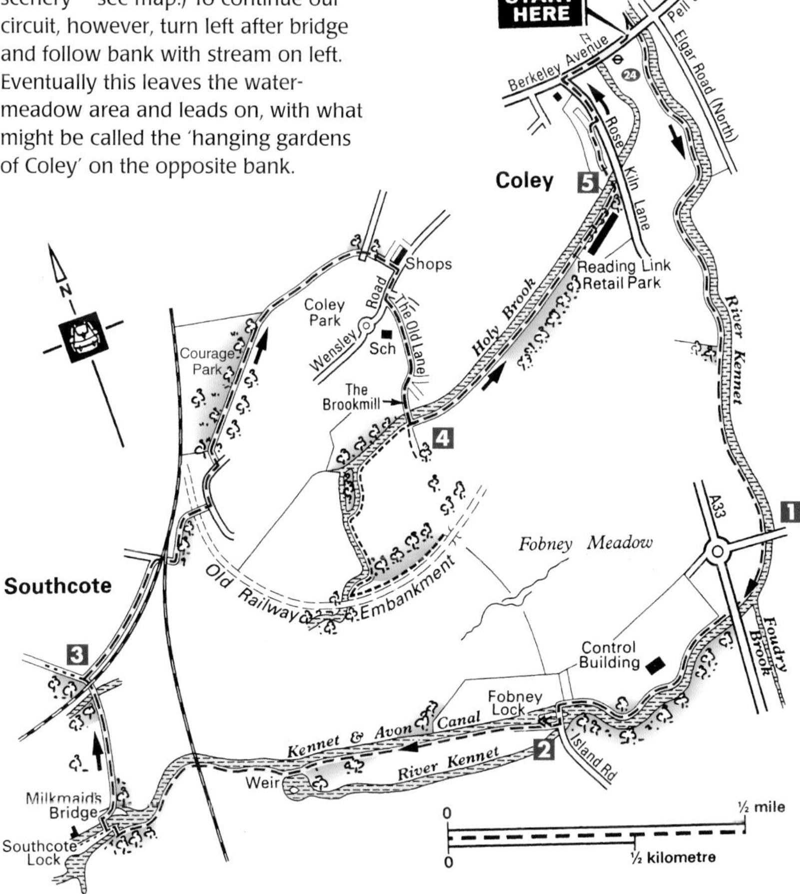

Chill Hill and Jouldings Farm

Explore some quiet tucked-away corners of rural scenery in the parishes of Swallowfield and Finchampstead, with glimpses of the secretive River Blackwater, on the Berkshire/Hampshire boundary.

Distance: 5 miles
OS Map: Explorer 159 Reading
Start: Entrance to King George's Field, Castle Road, Farley Hill. (Grid ref: 752 644)

With your back to King George's Field, go left along road until, about 100 yards beyond bend in road, turn right into narrow Church Lane. At end of Cricket Club field turn left into fenced path and follow field on right to road. Now turn left along this quiet lane. At crossroads, Bunce's Shaw, go straight on and where lane swings left, keep straight ahead, now on shingle surfaced track. Where this turns off, still go straight on (a public byway).

1 Pass 'Badgers Wood' and just before track bears right, look out for start of footpath on left beside drive gateway. Follow path down through trees, soon beside field on left. At path junction turn left along broad hedged byway (Cordery's Lane) and at road junction carry on ahead, up Bunglers Hill, keeping to verge where possible.

2 When level with end of field on right, turn right into hedged byway (Raggetts Lane). Look for path on left at start of second field. Turn left through metal posts and follow path bearing left then head directly up open field to top boundary. From this point (Chill Hill) the Reading skyline reveals Shire Hall, the Madejski Stadium and the wind turbine. Walk down slope, with trees on left, and cross footbridge on left into meadow. Now aim towards house beyond distant tree, along level mid-field line.

3 On far side of field at stile by gate,

A sheltered setting at Farley Hill

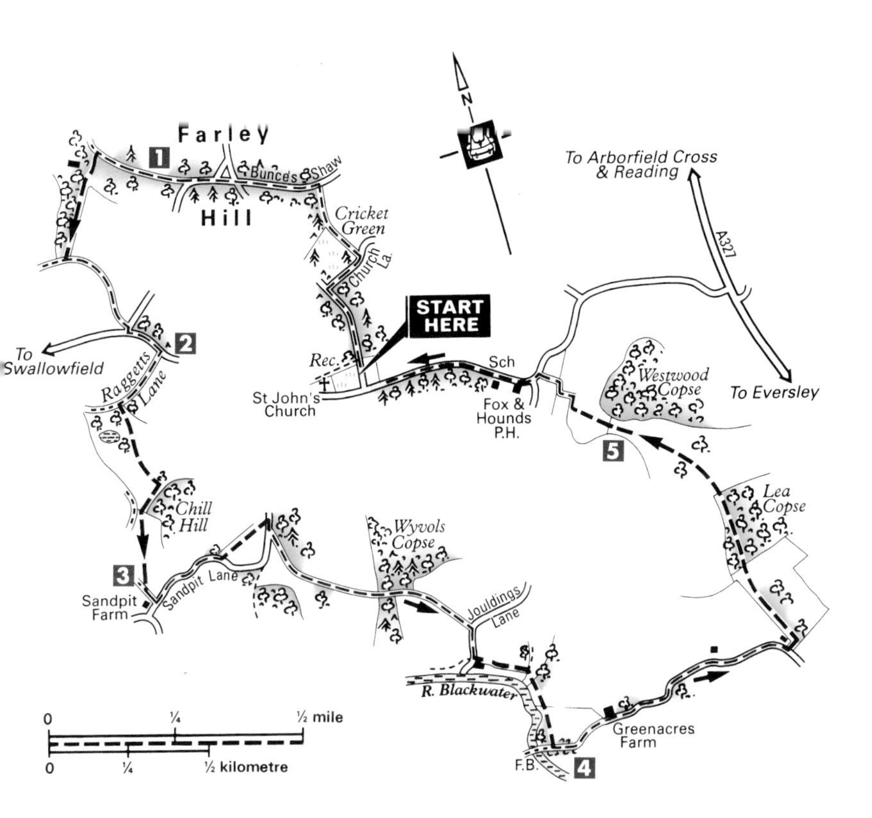

join wide grass track ahead and turn left up road (Sandpit Lane). Where lane dips down, look for footpath climbing steps up bank on left. With hedge on left at first, follow path down to road and turn right for some 40 yards, then bear left into byway. Follow this to its far end then turn right down lane and turn left over footbridge, through kissing gate and alongside fence. (signed Blackwater Valley Path). From kissing gate go half-right to gate in corner then over stile and continue with fence on right. Cross two stiles, linking fields and where fence on right swings away towards river (Blackwater), bear left to pass mid-field trees, to reach stile in hedgerow.

4 Turn left along hedged grass track and after kissing gate bear left, soon passing Greenacres Farm. Continue, now on tarmac roadway, past thatched Bulloway's Farm until, just beyond sharp right-hand bend, turn left through metal gate into short track beside Lea Cottage. Turn left entering field and keep to left side of two fields ahead, then through trees (Lea Copse). Cross hand-railed footbridge and continue ahead, past pylon, on midfield line, to stile beside gates, at far end of big field.

5 Definitive path now goes straight on, diagonally across lower half of field, towards two oak trees. Here bear right up field-edge and in a few yards go up bank and turn left over stile. Enclosed path climbs, then turns right into garden, beside lawn, then left, to follow line of conifers to road. Turn left, then shortly right, passing 'Fox & Hounds', along footway on left side of road back to start.

DATE WALKED

Lower Shiplake and the Lock

Take this opportunity to add a whole loop of unspoilt Thames scenery opposite Wargrave to an existing length above Shiplake Lock, before climbing the bluff to Shiplake Church.

Distance: 4½ miles
OS Map: Explorer 159 Reading
Start: Playing-field car park at Memorial Hall, Memorial Ave., Shiplake. (Grid ref: 764 787)

If parking several cars, please check beforehand with hall – tel: (0118) 940 3303

Turn right out of car park and follow splendid rows of maple trees along Memorial Avenue. At Shiplake Cross, with great care cross main road and go 30 yards along Mill Lane before bearing left into steadily descending, unmade New Road. Go straight on at crossing, soon to reach junction with lane (Mill Road).

1 At a public inquiry in 2009 sufficient evidence of uninterrupted public use was presented by the RA to convince the inspector that previous landowners had deemed to dedicate the route ahead as a public right of way.*

Cross Mill Road into drive ahead, to left of Virginia Cottage. Pass the quaint Lashbrook Chapel. Keep right of wooden-panel fence ahead. Cross stile and bear left along field edge and pass through wild area and under railway viaduct (mind your 'ead!) with stiles either side. Now look half-right for path across watermeadows ahead, to cross wooden footbridge, leading to riverbank. (The old Lashbrook ferry-point is just down-stream).

2 Turn right along towpath, passing a variety of properties on far bank, dominated by Wargrave Manor (presently owned by the Sultan of Oman) perched in hilltop splendour, floodlit at night. Concrete steps mark point of another old ferry to 'George & Dragon' on Wargrave bank. (See map for alternative route here, back through open fields). Ahead lies the iron viaduct (built 1897 to replace a wooden structure) carrying the single-track branch line to Henley-on-Thames. Go under main span and follow the right of way ahead, through series of riverside gardens. In the last of these, with wooden boathouse ahead, turn right to pass left of property (Rivermead Cottages) and turn left along Mill Lane.

3 At end of brick and flint wall of Mill House turn left down tarmac path to visit Shiplake Lock. To continue, go through swing-gate off lock path and through riverside meadows ahead, open at first, then beside fence, between white-painted Shiplake House above and, in mid-stream, Phillimore's Island. Path along river's edge leads through wooded strip before opening onto lawned area at landing-stage of Shiplake College, standing high above here, behind the trees.

Grazing the riverside path